Inside the Big Band Drum Chart

Steve Fidyk

Online Audio & Video

Audio
www.melbay.com/21475MEB

Video
dv.melbay.com/21475

You Tube
www.melbay.com/21475V

The audio recording contains demonstrations of all the exercises and arrangements featured in the book.

The titles for each exercise and arrangement listed in the book are organized using an MP3 icon.
Each exercise and arrangement coincides with the titles on the audio recording.

1 2 3 4 5 6 7 8 9 0

Visit us on the Web at www.melbay.com — E-mail us at email@melbay.com

Foreword from Peter Erskine

Buddy Rich once remarked that the drum fill played by Shadow Wilson on the Count Basie Orchestra tune "Queer Street" was the "most perfect drum break ever recorded." Steve Fidyk's book, "Inside The Big Band Drum Chart" is the first book I know of that includes a transcription of this momentous fill, along with several generations' worth of innovative drum fills, all within the context of a learning method that will teach any interested drummer how to practice the art of reading, playing time and connecting big band phrases together.

The big band is where most jazz players of note got their start. For years it was the entryway for young musicians to enter the music "biz." And while times have changed, there's nothing that can compare to the excitement of a big band or to the invaluable ensemble playing experience that big bands offer. Every drummer can benefit from knowing how to play arranged music. Fortunately, Steve's book comprehensively covers both traditional and contemporary ground.

The best way to learn any style of music is to LISTEN. "Inside The Big Band Drum Chart" includes access to online audio (with 59 tracks!) as well as a discography of recommended listening. This excellent method book and audio combination offers instructional text, music examples, plus play-along and listening tracks that should prove invaluable for young players, aspiring professionals and "weekend warriors" who want to experience the thrill of sitting in the driver's seat of a big band. Steve Fidyk comes well qualified to provide all of these things. He has been the drummer for the excellent U.S. Army Blues big band for many years, as well as the co-leader of a terrific big band with arranger and composer Mark Taylor. I've shared several drum class podiums with Steve, and know him to be a fully qualified and effective teacher as well as a world-class player (Steve also transcribed some of my work for one of my own books). He is a conscientious educator; this book was ten years in the making. I am proud to be able to write these words of introduction to "Inside the Big Band Drum Chart," especially because any book that has that phenomenal Shadow Wilson break in it deserves our utmost attention and respect!

~ Peter Erskine

Welcome to *Inside the Big Band Drum Chart*, a book of exercises and ideas to help improve chart reading and interpretation. In this method, the music is the vehicle providing a format to study beats, form, ensemble phrasing, and interpretation. For each arrangement, I discuss my approach, provide transcriptions of key beats and band figure examples, and "talk through information" explaining how each composition is played.

In order for this material to have musical significance, it's essential to listen to master big band drummers like Jo Jones, Dave Tough, Gene Krupa, Buddy Rich, Mel Lewis, and Jake Hanna. From this experience, you will begin to understand that this musical style requires far more from a drummer than mere reading ability. Contemporary big band drummers have strong time and an awareness of the form and melody as they supply the accompaniment for the bands' articulation, phrasing, and dynamics.

Hopefully this method will get you started swinging in a big band as I provide insight to what reading a chart is like.

The accompanying recording contains audio demonstrations of each exercise. Also included are two complete versions of the six arrangements. Version one is the reference listening track with drums, and version two is a play-along track without drums. I recommend you listen to the reference tracks first before practicing with the play-along. This will ensure an accurate performance while guiding you in developing your reading confidence and interpretive skills.

The video will help complete the puzzle with my personal views, drumming tips, and musical performances of each of the six arrangements.

The Musicians

Lucas Munce	*Alto and soprano sax, flute, clarinet*
Andy Axelrad	*Alto sax, flute, clarinet*
Tedd Baker	*Tenor sax, flute, clarinet*
Dave Stump	*Tenor sax, flute, clarinet*
Doug Morgan	*Baritone sax, flute, and bass clarinet*
Brian MacDonald	*Lead Trumpet*
Kevin Burns	*Split Lead*
Rich Sigler	*Trumpet, flugel*
Tim Leahey	*Trumpet, flugel*
Ryan Haines	*Tenor and bass trombone*
Ben Patterson	*Tenor trombone*
Jeff Martin	*Tenor trombone*
Todd Hanson	*Bass trombone*
Jim Roberts	*Guitar*
Tony Nalker	*Piano*
Paul Henry	*Bass*
Steve Fidyk	*Drums*
Regan Brough	*Bass on the 12 bar blues, 32 bar song form, and tempo transition exercise*

Recorded and mixed at
BIAS Studios, Springfield, VA

Engineers:
Bob Dawson
Craig Lauinger
Jim Robeson

Produced by **Steve Fidyk**

Acknowledgements

I would like to thank Bill Bay, Julie Price, and all of the wonderful people at Mel Bay Publications for allowing me the opportunity to share my teaching ideas and experiences. To Ryan Haines who composed and arranged the music and Danny Behr, President of Walrus Music Publishing for allowing these arrangements to be featured in the book. The complete band tracks were taken from Ryan's two solo CD's that I was fortunate enough to be a part of: *New Horizons and People and Places*. Both recordings are available through Sea Breeze Records. I'd also like to thank Bill Miller at Modern Drummer Magazine for the quotes and everyone at Zildjian for the photos.

Thanks to my brother Bill for editing the text and to all of the legendary musicians who were so gracious and giving of their time with the interviews at the back of the book. An extra special thanks to my wife Tamela and sons Tony and Joey for their support and patience during the making of this project and for keeping my life centered with love.

Contents

Set Up The Band! _____ page

Preliminary Charts _____

Big Band Arrangements with Analysis _____

Appendix _____

Drum Set Notation

This section explains the many notational signs and abbreviations arrangers use in big band drum parts. We begin with the Notation Key below.

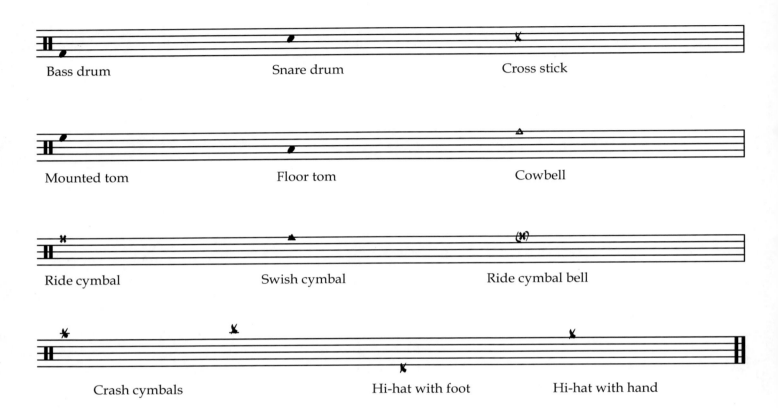

Bass drum	Snare drum	Cross stick
Mounted tom	Floor tom	Cowbell
Ride cymbal	Swish cymbal	Ride cymbal bell
Crash cymbals	Hi-hat with foot	Hi-hat with hand

• = closed

o = open

ø = 1/2 open

The Chart Talk Through

Details concerning ensemble and section entrances, repeated sections, style, form, phrasing, and dynamics are all answered during the chart talk through. This information is critical when playing a chart for the first time. I have a pencil in hand when these directions are given by the conductor or band leader and make notes on my part that help me when reading. Talk through information is given for each arrangement in this text.

Big Band Forms

Recognizing a composition's form will help you learn an arrangement faster, as you develop the confidence to stop looking at the drum part. You can determine any songs' form by listening for musical statements that repeat.

The two most common big band forms are the blues and the 32 measure song form (AABA).

The blues form is 12 measures long, divided into three phrases. Each 12-measure interval is a chorus. It is typical in a blues for the melody to be played twice.

The second is the 32 measure song form (AABA). Many popular songs, including numerous Broadway show tunes from the 1930's and 40's utilize this layout. The opening statement (A) is eight measures establishing the melody and harmony. It is then repeated, creating the second phrase. The next statement is in a new key and is also eight measures (B). This phrase is often referred to as the bridge, channel, or release. Finally, the last phrase is a repeat of the first statement (A).

Below are the arrangements and song forms featured throughout the book.

- Blaine Street (funk/AAB 8+8+8)
- Bottom End Shuffle (swing shuffle/12 bar blues)
- Good Night Story (ballad/ABAB/8+8+8+8)
- Swing Open (medium swing/12 bar blues)
- Tierrasanta (samba/AABA/8+8+16+8)
- People and Places (fast swing/ABA/8+8+8)

Reading and Interpreting Ideas

To coin an old adage, "reading is fundamental," to fully enjoy this book, reading written notation is a prerequisite. If you need help in this area, seek instruction from a reputable teacher and visit the drum method's discography at the back of this book for a recommended reading list.

There *is not* a standardized method that arrangers use for writing drum parts. Some composers give exact information concerning style, tempo, important ensemble or section accents, and sometimes suggested beats for certain sections of a chart. I've also read charts that provided nothing more than the name of the composition followed by numerous measures of repeat signs. A drum chart does not accurately represent what you play, instead, it is a guide that drummers use to *improvise* and *compose* an individual part. This is the greatest difference between brass or reed parts and a drum part.

Another point is that most arrangers are not drummers and often have difficulty communicating exactly what they expect from you on the part. One suggestion would be to question what you see and listen carefully as you read. Listen for the ensemble's phrasing (swung or straight), articulations (long or short), and dynamics (loud or soft) and use this information to help compose appropriate beats and figure interpretation.

When reading, always concentrate on your time and keep it consistent as you hold the arrangement together. This is far more important than "kicking" every accent on the drum part.

When reading any arrangement, take a moment and think about what the audience is listening for. Try directing their attention to "landmark" elements as the composition unfolds: the introduction, melody, solos and backgrounds, shout choruses, etc. As you read, listen for these signposts, which together make up the entire puzzle. Interpreting music in this manner can help bring about a more effective accompaniment plan. Your personal interpretation of the music should reflect the amount of detail found within the arrangement itself.

Internalizing the melody and its variations, the musical form of the composition (12 measure blues, AABA song), and the style of the arrangement (swing, funk, Latin, etc.), can help you interpret, improvise, and ultimately sound like you're contributing as an equal member of the ensemble.

An ensemble will follow the drummer's lead when performing dynamics. The dynamic approach to a phrase (loud or soft), begins with you! Experiment by exaggerating your softs and louds and see how the ensemble responds. Playing one dynamic throughout a composition forces the ensemble to do the same.

As you read band figure rhythms, your interpretation should enhance the flow and feel of the phrase. In many cases, an overuse of fills and set ups can detract from the forward momentum of the music.

Always think musically and be able to justify your musical choices. One example of this is when a musical theme ascends from a low register to a higher one, try playing the phrase by ascending from your low drum (bass drum or floor tom), to a higher voice (possibly snare drum or hi-hat). The written phrase on your drum part will not reflect any shape. You need to listen as you read to determine this, or consult the lead trumpet part to discover the shape of the musical line.

The section or ensemble articulation (long or short), should be represented in your style. When playing, or speaking for that matter, be as articulate as possible. By doing so, the ensemble will hear your ideas more clearly and ultimately play more accurately.

Engage the listener with ideas that have variety and contrast as you lead the ensemble through each musical phrase.

Listening exercise:

Listen to the reference recording, or put on one of your favorite big band recordings and listen for the main sections of the arrangement: introduction, melody, solos and backgrounds, shout chorus, etc. Next, try and determine the form of the composition. This may take several listen throughs to solve. Once you know where these landmarks are in the music, think about ways of interpreting them. Also consider how you might rhythmically transition from one section to the next. Use information you hear within the rhythm section and brass and reed sections to come up with beat and fill ideas. Jot these ideas down on a separate sheet of paper and begin practicing with the recording.

"The drummers should be sitting up there knowing the music inside and out. There is no reason to be sitting there reading anything. The reading should have been done at the first rehearsal, maybe the second or third rehearsals, maybe even the fourth rehearsal. After that they shouldn't even be looking at the music. They should know the part, and they should be just listening and finding the inside of everything."

Mel Lewis, Modern Drummer, February 1985.

Rhythmic Interpretation

The following interpretation is commonly accepted when performing eighth note rhythms in a swing style. This interpretation produces a smooth, connected, legato feeling.

The tempo and style of a composition can also influence the way eighth notes are interpreted. Early swing music of the 1920's and 30's for example has a phrasing that is more closely related to this interpretation:

Arrangements played in a fast be bop style (300 beats per minute or faster), the eighth notes are interpreted and performed fairly straight:

There are no set rules that govern the way a particular phrase is to be swung. Each band has its own rhythmic feel and phrasing style. To recognize this, listen to the lead players (trumpet 1, trombone 1, and alto 1) and match their phrasing and accents.

Alternate Notation for Time

Big band drummers supply articulate time, sound, and dynamics as they compose beats and fills appropriate to the musical style. In many cases however, the most musical beat or fill option is not the written rhythm on your part; it is provided as a suggestion, and since most arrangements are not written by drummers, composers tend to "leave room" for one's personal interpretation.

A drum chart can vary in its detail. Many parts contain suggested beats, fills, dynamics, and a clear format. On the other hand, some parts are merely sketches with select brass, reed, and ensemble cues. This can be problematic for an inexperienced player not familiar with reading and interpreting charts since much of the notation and abbreviations used are not always obvious.

The following pages illustrate the most frequently used abbreviations for time in big band drum parts.

Slash Notation

When notated with a style indicator like the example below, slash notation acts as a substitute for the written beat. This "short hand" approach means to play time in the appropriate style of the composition and is very common. You will find it in the Preliminary Charts and play along drum parts throughout the book. In a 4/4 time signature, one slash equals one quarter note duration.

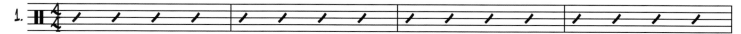

Slash notation can also be used to alert the performer to play a drum fill or solo over a set number of beats or measures. In example 2, the player is directed to fill for four beats as a "set up" for the ensemble figures in the following measure.

In cut time, each slash equals one half note duration.

If the composer has a suggested beat in mind, you will usually find it at the start of a new musical phrase followed by several bars of slash notation.

Suggested beat with slash notation:

Repeat Notation

Arrangers also use single measure repeat signs following a suggested beat indicating to play time. In either case, slash and repeat sign notation function the same.

Suggested beat with one measure repeat notation:

If the written drum beat consists of two measures, 2 measure repeat signs follow denoting to repeat the two measure suggested rhythm.

Phrase Notation

Example 7 is phrase notation that instructs the performer to play 8 measures of time in the appropriate style. You may also encounter "play 12" or "play 16" in various drum parts that you sight read. This method helps save space on the part.

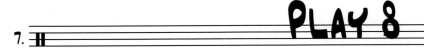

7.

Stock Notation

8.

Example 8 is "stock notation" found in older drum parts from the 1940's. This notation closely resembles a snare and bass drum part from a concert band percussion section. These swing arrangements were written specifically for dancing with no open or improvised sections.

Examples 9, 10, and 11 illustrate common interpretations for the stock notation in example 8.

Fox trot beat in 2:

Swing in 4 ex. 1:

Swing in 4 ex. 2:

Because interpretation is such a large part of big band drumming, it is essential to listen to the music you perform to understand the style and musical concept.

Your approach to a stock arrangement will be different than that of a modern swing chart. If you haven't listened to the music, you will have a difficult time accompanying the ensemble in a musical way.

For Terminology Purposes Only!!

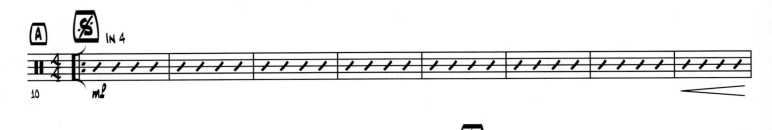

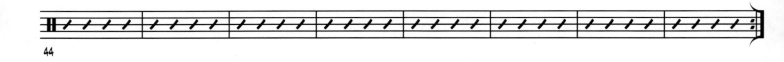

Basic Chart Reading Terminology

The chart "For Terminology Purposes Only" contains many terms, signs, and abbreviations as they appear on a drum part. It serves as a primer to help acquaint you with many common terms and signs that arrangers use.

Below is a phrase by phrase look pointing out each and explaining their meanings.

For the terms and abbreviations not covered in this chart, I've included a listing of additional terms and definitions that you may find in a reading situation.

1. *Style Marking.* Indicates the musical style of the composition

2. *Tempo Marking.* The tempo the composition is to be performed at

3. *FF.* Fortissimo--very loud

4. *Pick Up Measure.* Information written to the left of the double bar line. Pick up measures are usually the first measure of the piece with the count off occurring within this bar.

5. *Ensemble Figures with articulation marks.* Notation played by the entire ensemble that is normally written within the staff. Articulation marks are notated above specific rhythms to signal note duration and intensity.

6. *Eyeglasses.* Used in arrangements to draw attention to a specific measure or phrase

7. *Double Barline.* Marks the end of a phrase

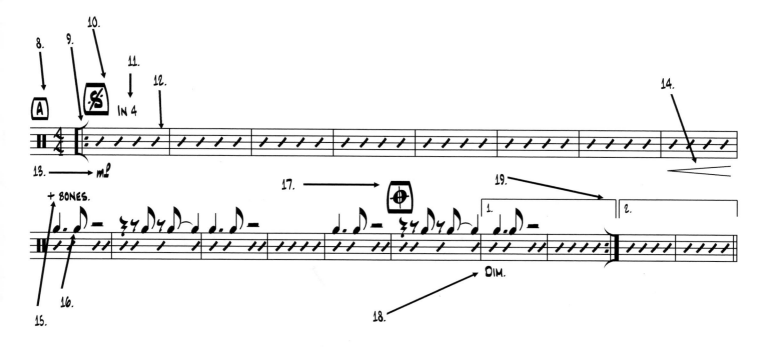

8. *Rehearsal Letter.* Rehearsal letters or numbers locate major sections of a composition

9. *Repeat Signs.* The measures located between the dotted bar lines are to be repeated

10. *D.S. or Dal Segno.* Return to the sign

11. *In 4.* Play a beat with a feeling of 4 beats to the measure

12. *Slash Notation.* This is alternate notation that is an abbreviation for playing time. Each slash indicates one quarter note duration in 4/4.

13. *mp.* Mezzo Piano--moderately soft

14. *Crescendo sign.* Gradually get louder

15. **+ Bones.** Added trombone backgrounds

16. **Background Figures.** Notation written above the staff played by a section of the band.

17. **Coda Sign.** When you see this sign, jump to the coda phrase located at the end of the drum part.

18. **Dim.** Diminuendo--gradually get softer

19. **1st and second ending repeat signs.** When reading these repeated endings, play through the 1st ending the first time through the music and repeat back to the opposite facing repeat sign. When you repeat the music the second time, the second ending will be played instead of the first.

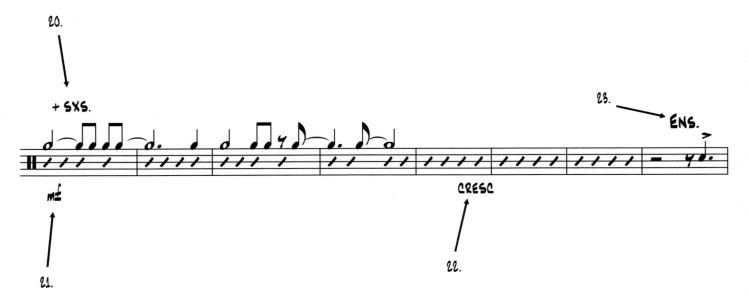

20. **+ SXS.** Added saxophone background figures

21. **mf.** Mezzo Forte. Moderately loud

22. **CRESC.** Gradually get louder

23. **ENS.** Ensemble entrance

24. **Open Solos.** When marked "open", repeat the solo section until you are directed to
play the next phrase of music. Often, solo sections have a fixed number of times
to be repeated. For example, 4X. When you see this marking, the music
is to be repeated a total of 4 times.

25. **Decrescendo sign.** Gradually get softer

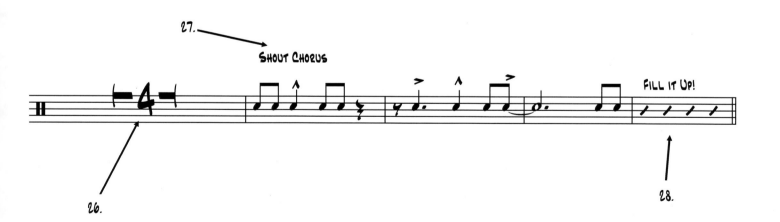

26. *Multi Measure Rest.* Rest for four measures

27. *Shout Chorus.* Dynamically, the loudest and most intense section of an arrangement

28. *Fill it Up.* Play a solo fill for one measure

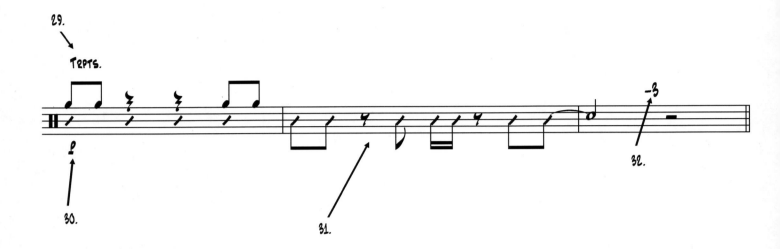

29. *Trpts.* Trumpet section

30. *p.* Piano--softly

31. *Rhythmic Notation.* Play rhythm in unison or tutti with the ensemble without fills producing an effect that is crisp and punchy

32. *-3.* Cut off or release the held note on beat 3

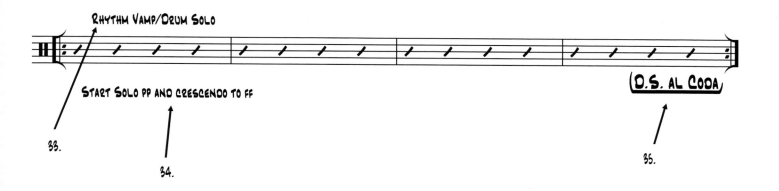

33. **Rhythm Vamp/Drum Solo.** Play an open drum solo over a repeated vamp established by the rhythm section. This short phrase is played until directed to take the D.S.

34. ***pp and crescendo to ff.*** Begin the drum solo pianissimo (very soft), and gradually get louder to ff (fortissimo)

35. **D.S. Al Coda.** Once the drum solo is complete, take the D.S. AL Coda by returning to measure 10. Next, read the music up to where the coda sign appears (the end of measure 23), and then jump to the coda (measure 74), and play the arrangement until the end.

36. **The Coda.** The coda phrase is the final section of an arrangement. It is designed to bring a composition to a close.

37. **Rit.** Ritard--gradually slow down

38. **Fermata Sign.** Hold the note longer than its written duration; Tempo is suspended and resumed on cue

39. **Railroad tracks.** Abruptly stop the music and the preceding note is cued

Below are additional terms not found in "For Terminology Purposes Only", which you may come across when reading a piece of music:

DA CAPO (D.C.) Return to the beginning of the composition, read up to the coda sign, then jump to the coda

Segue. Transition immediately to the next section of music without a pause

L'istesso. Same tempo

A Tempo. Play the phrase at the original tempo

Accelerando. Speed up the tempo

Ad lib. Improvise

Dictated. Each beat is conducted

DBL X. Transition to a tempo that is twice as fast

1/2 X. Transition to a tempo that is half as fast

Simile. Continue the same pattern

Soli. A written and arranged solo played by a section of the band

Rall. Rallentando--to slow down the tempo

Tacet. Do not play the marked phrase. This is sometimes indicated by drawing a circle around the notes to be taceted.

In 1. A fast tempo where the pulse of the composition is one beat to the measure.

In 2. In 4/4 time, the half note receives the pulse. The rhythm is felt with a basic pulse of two beats per measure with emphasis on beats 1 and 3.

Time Keeping Elements

The following section individually examines the role of the primary timekeeping sounds of the bass drum, hi-hat, and ride cymbal. Developing a consistent technique on each instrument will affect the beats and fills you play as you combine your limbs together. Try practicing each instrument from your drum set individually.

Creating a consistent sound on one surface is the first step to developing uniformity on a multi-surface instrument. Use the 12 measure blues bass track and the 32 measure song form bass track on the audio and strive for consistency with the rhythms you play and the sounds you produce.

The Bass Drum

The bass drum is the foundation of your swing feel. It can be used to keep time by feathering four quarter notes to the measure, or used for accenting rhythms played by the ensemble. The bass drum sound is an essential element that helps drive a big band and provides depth and range to your time feel. Throughout the 1920's and 30's, the bass drum was the anchor of the rhythm section beating four quarter notes to the bar. Today it's a soft pulse you want to obtain with the acoustic bass. A controlled quarter note pulse on the bass drum in sync with the walking acoustic bass line will augment the ensembles sound and reinforce the swing feel. How hard you swing is determined by the movement of your feet and the dynamic in which you play your bass drum and hi-hat pedals. A quarter note pulse played too loudly on the bass drum can create a heavy feel that has little propulsion or forward momentum.

Sounds of the Bass Drum

Heel Down- Feathering Technique (Ballad or Medium Swing)

Accenting Techniques:

a. Heel down Rebounding
b. Heel down Non Rebounding

c. Heel up Rebounding
d. Heel up Non Rebounding

The hi-hat can function as a timekeeper with sticks as you coordinate how open and closed the cymbals are, or for strengthening beats two and four of your ride cymbal pattern with your left foot.

Drummers Jo Jones of the Count Basie Band and Ray McKinley of the Glenn Miller Band are the "fathers" of the hi-hat. Listening to recordings of them play will provide the example for excellent hi-hat technique. Both players could swing a band for an entire arrangement by opening and closing and varying the playing area on the cymbals. The key to creating a sound is for the top and bottom cymbals to always touch. As your left foot rests on the pedal board, slightly lift your toes raising the cymbals. This will give you a small opening between the cymbals which is enough to make a sound. If you open them a little more, this produces a louder sound. Playing the hi-hat is an art form all to itself.

Sounds of the hi-hat

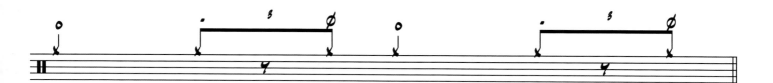

- Beats 1 and 3 are open with both cymbals still touching.
- Beats 2 and 4 the cymbals are closed. This is achieved with your left foot or by using your left hand to mute the cymbals.
- The "a" of 2 and 4, the cymbals are half open, a tension between closed and open.

The hi-hat sound should lead to the prominent or open beats of 1 and 3.

The Ride Cymbal

The ride cymbal (or top cymbal as it was originally called) is used for backing soloists and for loud ensemble accompanying. For modern music, a good ride cymbal will have a balance of stick attack and overtones or ring.

The ride cymbal is the most important element for achieving a good flowing swing feel and by accenting the quarter note pulse within your ride pattern will help "lock in" your three remaining limbs when playing time.

Knowing where the quarter note is and how it relates to the rhythms you are playing will help develop solid time, regardless of what style of music you are playing.

Sounds of the Ride Cymbal

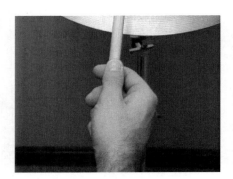

Staccato Sounds
a. Close to the Bell
b. In the bell

Legato Sounds
a. Near the edge
b. Shoulder crashes at the edge of the cymbal
c. Suspended cymbal rolls with mallets

The following page demonstrates the three most common ways of phrasing the ride cymbal beat. The phrasing I'm referring to occurs on the 2nd and 4th beats of the measure. Example one shows the phrasing as a dotted eighth and sixteenth note grouping. Example two produces a looser feel because the phrasing is based on an eighth note triplet grouping. The third example shows how the ride beat is phrased at a very fast tempo of 300 beats per minute or faster.

Ride Cymbal Phrasing Examples

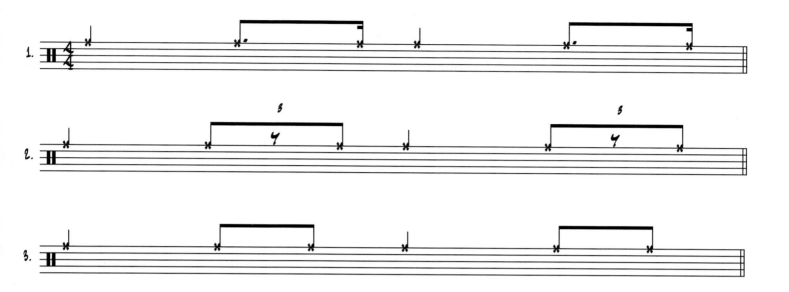

Swingin' and the Groove (two and four/one and three)

There has been much discussion about the feeling of the swing pulse and what beats in the measure are most important. Some consider two and four essential, while others groove off of one and three. Consider this; the strong beats in a measure are one and three, with the weaker beats being two and four emphasized by your hi-hat. The feeling of swing is generated in part by this relationship of strong to weak beats. As you swing on the drum set, try creating a consistent 4 feel between your ride cymbal, bass drum (playing the quarter note lightly!), and the hi-hat on beats 2 and 4. Where you place the two and four in relation to the one and three will create a feeling; on top of the beat, on the beat, or laid back behind the beat.

Articulation Markings and Musical Shape

Articulation Markings

The following articulation symbols are common in horn parts. They are used as indicators for emphasis.

This symbol (-) signifies a long attack

(.) or (^) suggests a short attack

An accent (>) can be interpreted long or short depending upon the style and context.

As drummers, we cannot play note durations with the accuracy of a horn player, but we can designate sound sources from the drum set that best complement the articulation and intensity of a note or phrase.

A note's articulation when played on the drum set is determined by:

a. what section of the band is playing
b. the intensity of the phrase
c. the instrument range (high or low) the phrase is played

The key is to let your ears point you in the right musical direction. Your approach to phrasing and articulating should always complement the ensemble and by reading and understanding these symbols and their meanings, you will bring clarity to the longer phrases you play.

Below is an example showing a trumpet 1 phrase with articulation marks from the arrangement Swing Open, measures 67-74.

If we expose the rhythms with articulations, we have a phrase that illustrates the *emphasized* horn rhythms. These are destination points in a musical line that create a second tier of accent texture. With just the articulated rhythm, the phrase looks like this:

Below is one common drum set articulation for this phrase.

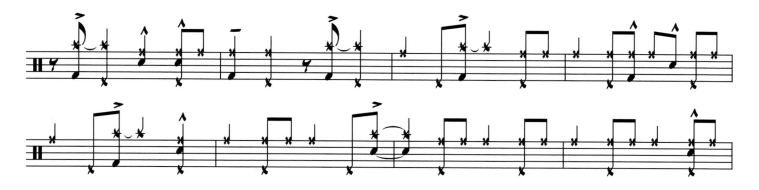

By reading and emphasizing the articulated rhythm, you naturally attain the notes a horn player gives significance to. *Now* you are phrasing and articulating with the band!!

Dynamic Expression and Shape

Each note we play has a dynamic. Percussionists achieve dynamic diversity through their stroke, motion, and stick direction. The closer the sticks are to the instrument when we begin our stroke, the softer the attack will be. Conversely, a stroke played further away from the drum produces a louder dynamic.

The speed or velocity used when we throw the stick to the instrument can also influence the way a phrase is felt and heard. A faster stick velocity can produce rhythms with more intensity and forward momentum. As you practice, try varying your stick height and velocity and listen carefully to the differences

in dynamic inflection. This approach can help bring expression to the written notation.

Music of all styles or genres has shape. As a piece of music develops, phrases ascend with intensity or descend creating different musical textures and moods. As you read, you will notice that drum parts from big band arrangements have a multitude of single "flat line" rhythms that do not indicate shape.

The top of the following page has an example of this from measures 39 and 40 from the drum part of Bottom End Shuffle. Does the musical line ascend or descend??? It's impossible to tell by observing the drum part alone.

Flat line drum set section figure example:

Below are the same two measures from the trumpet one part:

The line drawing below approximates the shape of the above multiple note trumpet figure. You can try this by drawing an imaginary line through each note head in a phrase and mirror the shape on the drums and cymbals.

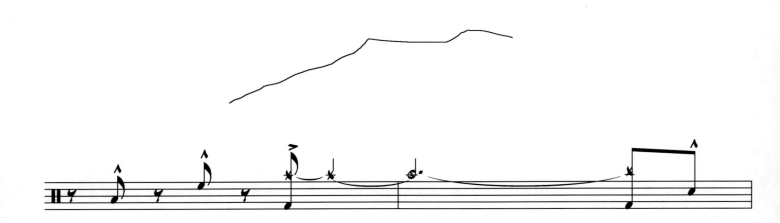

Short Articulation Exercise with Quarter Notes

This section provides exercises for reading and interpreting rhythms with short articulations. The top staff illustrates the way the figure would appear on a drum part. The bottom staff is one interpretation to that figure. I encourage you to use your imagination and creativity to come up with other ways to interpret the rhythm. The only guideline I would suggest is to dynamically balance the articulated note with the constant flowing sounds of the ride cymbal and hi-hat.

Short Articulation Exercise with Eighth Notes

40

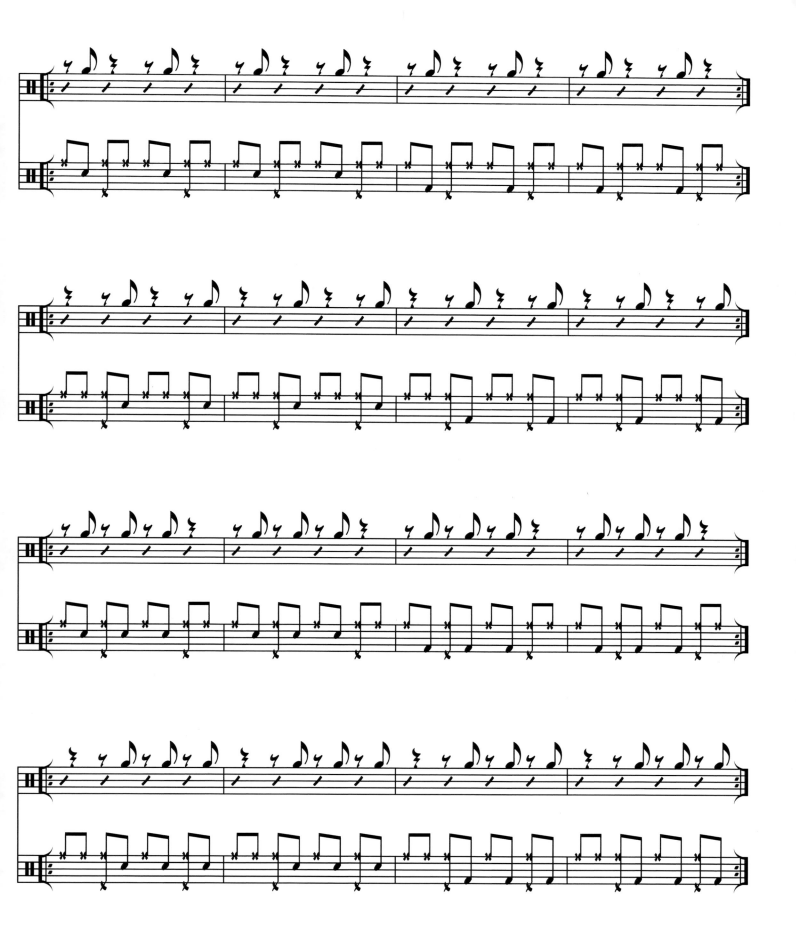

Short Articulation Exercise with Quarters and Eighth Notes

44

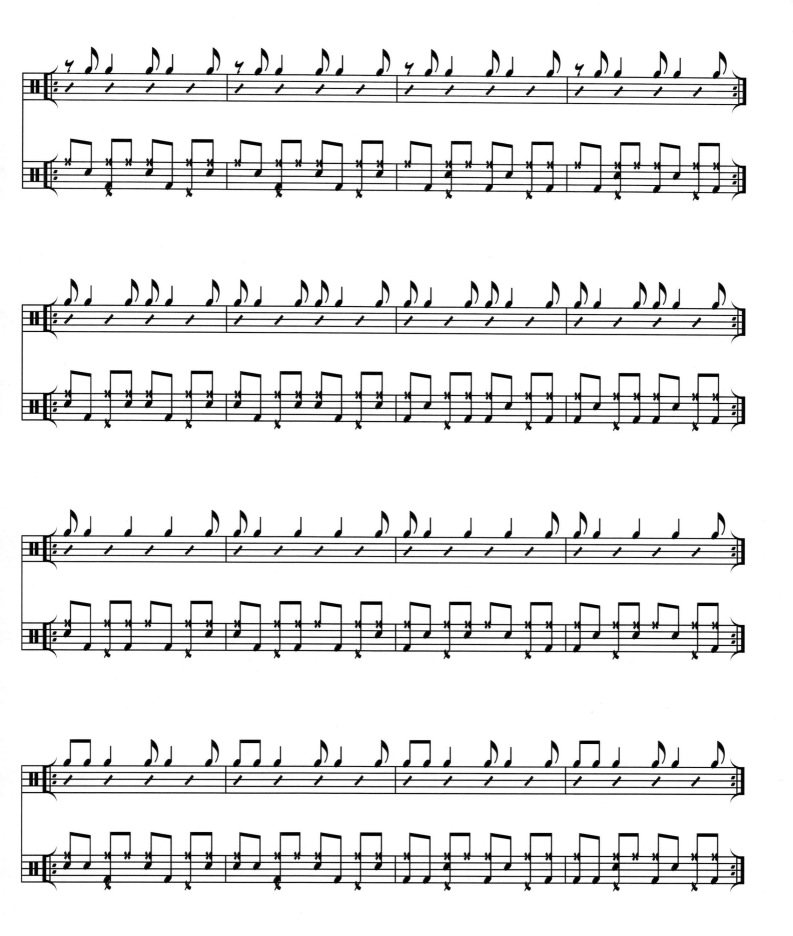

This exercise presents rhythms with long articulations. Like the previous collection, the top staff is how the rhythm would look on a drum part and the bottom staff is one way to interpret the rhythm. The ride cymbal pattern for each is varied to allow for movement to the crash cymbal and like the previous exercise, focus on blending the swing ride pattern with each long articulation. An over accented long articulation on a crash cymbal for example can negate the balance and flow of the time feel.

49

50

To experiment with fill set ups for these long figures, return to the first example and voice the ride cymbal rhythm on the snare drum or tom toms. The ride cymbal pattern as it is now written is the "connecting rhythm" between each figure. If the tempo is slow enough, further set ups can be performed using smaller subdivisions such as eighth note triplets or sixteenth notes. A faster tempo would require larger set up subdivisions such as eighth notes or quarter notes.

Also try this set up approach with the long and short articulation combination exercise.

Long and Short Articulation Combinations Example 1

Section and ensemble phrases are built on combinations of short and long attacks. This exercise mixes short and long articulations with the jazz ride cymbal pattern.

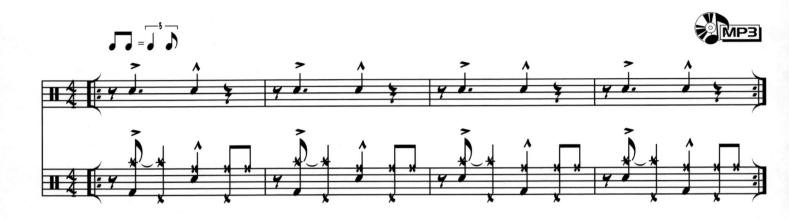

53

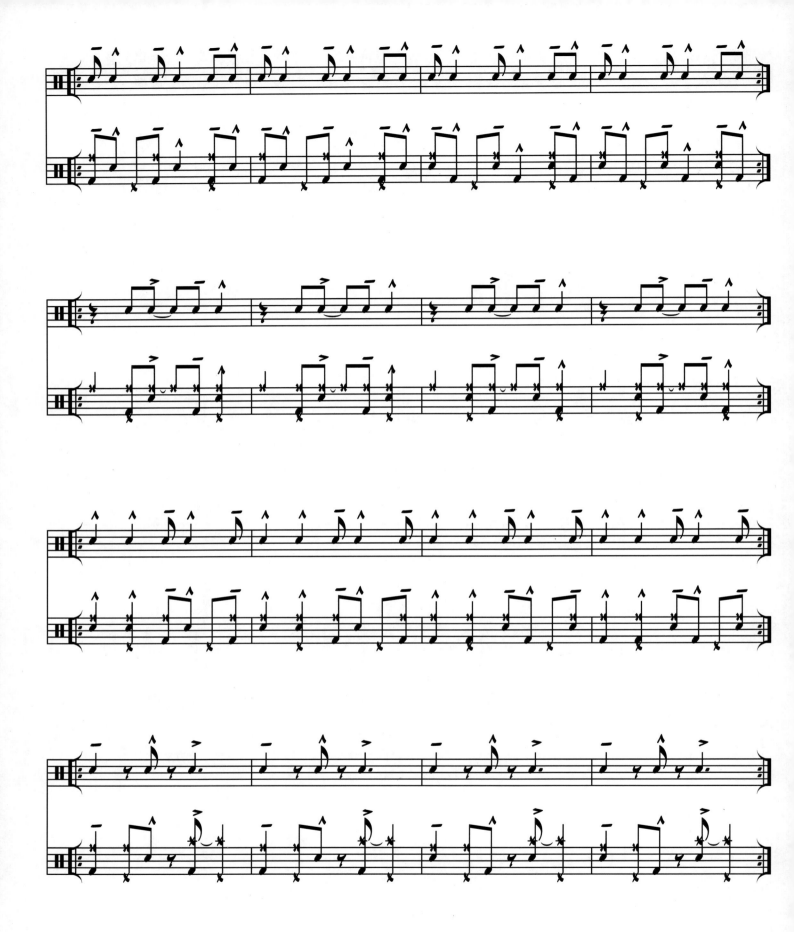

56

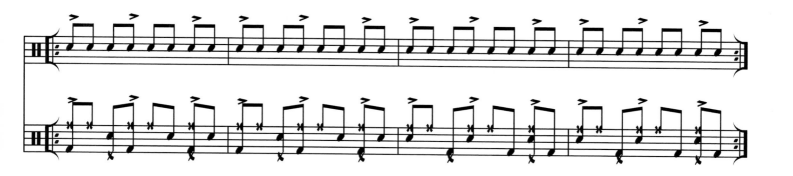

In rehearsal with Doc Severinsen

Contemporary Interpretation Exercise 1

When performing contemporary rock, funk or Latin music, the style hinges on the repetitive nature of the groove. For funk or rock, the backbeat on beats 2 and 4 and for Brazilian music, the samba rhythm played on the bass drum create the foundation. Playing fill set ups or beats that are busy can detract from the punchy stacatto effect that is desired when performing these styles.

Contemporary Interpretation Exercise 2

Further Application:

Now that you have completed the contemporary exercise with a funk approach, return to the first example and practice this collection as a Brazilian Samba Study. Your right foot will play the Samba pattern on the bass drum with beats two and four played with your left foot on the hi-hat. Your right hand can play eighth notes or any combination of sixteenth or eighth note patterns on the ride cymbal. Read the rhythms on the top staff with your left hand on the snare drum or tom toms.

The Big Band Sound

As drummers, our concern is to feel relaxed behind our instrument as we compose beats and accompany an arrangement. Some drummers develop their sound through years of experimentation, incorporating ideas that are influenced by the musicians they work with. Conversely, players sometimes stumble on a sound by accident not giving it much deliberation at all. Ideally, the musical style you're playing should dictate the drum and cymbal sound. Period music of the 1920's and 30's will require a different drum, cymbal set up, and tuning than a modern arrangement written in the later half of the 20th century for example.

In most bands, the drummer is sensitive to the *raw* sound of the drums and cymbals. Some players muffle their drums by putting a blanket inside of the bass drum shell or using duct tape on the tom heads because their prime concern is the sound as they hear it from behind the kit. The sound that travels and reaches the audience is the *projected* sound, or the sound that you should be concerned with. We can equate this concept of projection to hearing our own voice back on tape. Your recorded voice is the way you really sound as you speak but most people are not comfortable when hearing themselves back on tape. Do I really sound like that?? This concept holds true with drum timbre as well. Do you know how your drum set sounds out in front of your band? Ask yourself, why am I tuning this drum in this manner? Why am I playing time on this cymbal? Why am I playing this phrase at this dynamic? A logical answer is so that the audience and band members (that can sometimes be over 12 feet away from you) hear a clear, articulate tone. Always be able to justify your sound choices as they pertain to the music you make and musicians you accompany.

I strive for a projected sound that is *expansive* and open with minimal muffling, creating a balance between attack and tone. Remember, out in front of the drums, you won't hear as many overtones as you would if you were striking from behind the kit. The tone from each individual instrument is what *carries* the sound off the stage. This may take some getting use to if you have prescribed to muffling over the course of your playing career.

For big band, a common set up consists of a 14X22 or 16X20 bass drum, 5X14 snare (wooden or metal shell), 8X12 or 9X13 mounted tom, and a 14X14 or 16X16 floor tom. Each drum is tensioned so it has a balance of tone and attack that blends with the rest of the drum set.

Tuning

The goal with tuning your drums is to produce an articulate drum sound that leads the ensemble comfortably through the arrangement as it intensifies.

I begin with the snare drum. I tension the bottom head between a major 2nd and perfect 4th higher then the top head. This gives the drum a full bodied tone with a crisp attack.

For the bass drum, I tension my batter side head until there are no wrinkles present around the outside diameter. With the front head, I match the pitch with the batter head and then turn each lug approximately half a turn producing a tone on the front that is slightly higher. To muffle, I use a 3" felt strip that rests against the inside of the batter head tucked over the bearing edge of the shell. Legendary drummer Dave Tough was famous for tearing newspaper up in strips inside his bass drum shell to muffle. Mel Lewis would take a piece of paper napkin and put it over on the side of the batter head and adhere it using pieces of scotch or masking tape to decrease the overtones. If the music you play requires more attack, try a bass drum pedal with a wooden or hard plastic beater. For less attack, a felt beater works great. In all cases, I strive for a low sound from the bass drum.

With the toms, I tension both heads to the same pitch and then bring up the top head slightly because that is the head that is played on and will naturally come down in pitch over time.

A good general rule of thumb concerning big band drum tuning is the larger the ensemble, the lower the pitch of the drums. Lower pitched drums seem to project and blend better with a large ensemble.

Drum Heads _____

All of the great big band recordings made before 1957 feature the sound of drums with calfskin heads. After Remo Beli invented the plastic head, most drummers out of convenience switched due to the difficulty in keeping calf in tune. On a hot, humid day, the tuning of the drum would be lower because of the moist air affecting the heads. During the winter when it was dry, the heads would become very tight forcing the player to wet the heads in order to play on them. Mel Lewis swore by calf heads and used them his entire career on the bass drum. Buddy Rich preferred plastic heads. Experiment with both types and decide for you what sound works best. Calf tends to respond with a slower rebound with a stick and can feel softer and less abrasive than plastic. It also sounds great on the batter side of the bass drum because it creates fewer overtones than its plastic counterpart. With calf, if the temperature and humidity are just right, you can get a *thud* sound from the bass drum that is unrivaled. Brushes also sound great

when playing on calf heads. The sound of the wire as it sweeps across the head feels different than plastic. The heads, if cared for, tend to last longer too.

Cymbals

The Ride Cymbal _____

Most ride cymbals range from 20-22" in diameter. When performing contemporary arrangements, your ride cymbal should be versatile having a combination of high and low overtones with good stick definition. This is critical because this cymbal provides the quarter note pulse and suitable subdivision for the musical style. If your ride is too thin and low in pitch, the cymbal will not be heard throughout the band. Consequently, a ride that is thick and heavy can make your time feel too staccato with an over abundance of ping.

The ride cymbal can also function as a crash depending on the situation. The bell or cup should produce a sound that slices through contemporary arrangements with brilliance.

Crash Cymbals _____

Some big band drummers use them and some choose not to. Buddy Rich played with two 18" crashes. Some players use a 16" to their left and an 18" to their right. In interviews I've read, Buddy Rich would keep the faster or thinner crash closest to the band. Gene Krupa set up this way too. This can help when you punctuate figures with the band because the *front* or attack of the note will be more clearly heard with less overtones. Another option is to use one hybrid cymbal such as a crash ride. They range from 18-20" in diameter and like the name implies, it sounds great when you ride on it, and opens up fast when you crash it. Each cymbal on your kit can be a ride or a crash depending on the instrument, or section of instruments you are accompanying. A heavier weight crash cymbal would be articulate enough to ride on, while a thinner ride cymbal would have crash qualities that respond at a medium fast rate when you strike the shoulder of the cymbal.

Hi-Hats _____

A pair of hi-hats, like your ride cymbal, should be versatile because they too provide the quarter note pulse and subdivision. The pair should sound full when played with sticks or with the foot. Hi-hat cymbals that are thick tend to have a good chick sound but do not blend well with the ensemble with sticks. On the other hand, if the hi-hat cymbals are too thin; they will not provide a sizeable chick sound with the foot. A standard pair will have a heavy bottom and a medium top and range from 13-15" in diameter. Before the late 1960's, when popular music grew increasingly louder, all cymbals were manufactured thinner. A pair of hi-hat cymbals at that time consisted of a medium bottom and a thin top. It wasn't until the Avedis Zildjian Company introduced the *New Beat* model consisting of a heavy bottom and a medium top to help meet the needs of the more aggressive and electric musical styles.

Chinese Cymbal _____

The Zildjian family began making cymbals in Turkey, approximately 400 years ago. The original cymbals looked like a modern day Chinese or Swish cymbal. They made them for the military and were used in battle with the Turks in the Middle Eastern area of Persia which today is Iran. Currently, many cymbal manufacturers are making great Chinese cymbals that are thin, with a raised playing edge, and a high bell profile. Legendary big band drummers such as Mel Lewis, Shelly Manne,

Sid Catlett, and Cozy Cole used them to generate a deep driving texture that is very unique and complementary to an ensemble. Dave Tough was the earliest drummer to bring the Chinese cymbal to prominence as a viable time keeping sound with Woody Herman's First Heard in the 1940's. Drummers who use Chinese cymbals usually install rivets in them. Drummer Jeff Hamilton uses 3 rivets in his cymbal while the Swish Knocker produced by the Avedis Zildjian Company has 20 rivets. A cymbal with more rivets will produce greater resonance or spread. The Chinese cymbal can vary in size from 18" to 24" in diameter.

Sticks _____

The drum stick is an extension of your hand and should feel comfortable when playing all styles of music. It is the conduit that vibrates the heads and cymbals. If too heavy, it can produce a sound that is less articulate on a ride cymbal. A stick that is too light might not provide enough power or momentum when supporting the ensemble. Some players prefer wood tip, others like the sound and reliability of a nylon tip. Mel Lewis used nylon tip sticks on thin, low pitched Turkish K Zildjian Cymbals. Buddy Rich preferred wood tips on a 20" medium Avedis Zildjian Ride.

A nylon tip can increase stick definition and bring out the high sounds from a cymbal. They also can produce a more articulate sound on a thinner, low pitched cymbal. If you're on a budget like most of us, nylon tip sticks will last longer.

A wood tip produces a warm, darker sound on the ride cymbal as it brings out the lower frequencies in a cymbal. The tips can chip from repetitive use however which will affect the amount of clarity from your ride beat.

With Ed Shaughnessy, PASIC 2003

Set Up the Band!

A "set up" is an improvised fill that helps prepare a section or ensemble entrance enhancing the flow and excitement of the arrangement. Set ups are determined in part by the tempo and style of the piece and can complement or contrast its parent band figure rhythmically or dynamically.

Below is a 4 measure phrase followed by various set up approaches at different tempos:

At a slow tempo, you can utilize smaller subdivisions such as eighth note triplets or sixteenth notes as connective material.

Pick up measures

At fast tempos, there is less time for rhythmic fill activity.

Now let's look at each phrase side by side for analysis purposes.

Example 1 Analysis/84 beats per minute

 a. This is an example of *parallel motion*. The triplet fill leads the ensemble to the and of one. The figure is then played in unison with the horns. The drums and horns move parallel to one another.
 b. Example B creates *counter point*. By accenting beat one of measure three, the drum fill produces a new rhythmic figure. The ensemble rhythm is not played in unison and the ensemble enters on beat two.
 c. This is another example of parallel motion with sixteenth note set up fills.
 d. Because the tempo is slow, example D illustrates figures with eighth note triplet *connector material*.

Example 2 Analysis/138 beats per minute

 e. parallel motion figure treatment with eighth notes
 f. counter point example with quarter notes creating new accents on: (beat four, measure two), and (beat one, measure three)
 g. parallel motion with triplet fills
 h. eighth notes played as connector material

Example 3 Analysis/260 beats per minute

 i. eighth note connector material
 j. parallel motion with a quarter note fill set up
 k. eighth notes played as connector material

To reiterate, the three basic ways of interpreting figures with set ups are:

1. *Parallel motion* - An improvised fill that leads the ensemble to their figure where a unison rhythm is created with the band. The drums and ensemble move parallel to one another.

2. *Counter point* - This set up approach creates a new accent rhythm "in the holes" of a phrase where the band is resting and breathing.

3. *Connector material* - The use of rhythmic subdivisions such as eighth notes, triplets, or sixteenth notes bringing a sense of cohesion to the horn figures.

More thoughts on set ups and band figure interpretation

A good band or section figure set up replicates the dynamic of the ensuing figure. This will ensure that the ensemble plays their entrance with confidence. This does not mean you need to fill and play every figure on the part! Too much "filling" diminishes the flow of the time, creating a harsh, one-dimensional texture.

Experiment with set ups that create counter point. Try this, when the ensemble is resting and *breathing*, play a new rhythmic idea that is not written on your drum part. Consider this: What if the ensemble is having difficulty with a phrase that you are setting up and about to play in unison with them? Playing figures with a band that is having problems playing together can cause more rhythmic chaos. In this instance, a simple counter point fill set up, coupled with good flowing time, will create a reference point for the band and help the ensemble lock into the groove.

Building a fill vocabulary for band figures

Building a fill vocabulary takes practice and patience. At one time or another, you've probably wondered how a drummer could sight read a big band arrangement on the spot and sound like they've played it for years. How do they do that?? Well, through years of playing experience, they've become so familiar with "common figures" in arrangements that they react automatically to them, eliminating the process of reading each note and deciding on a tonal and rhythmic conclusion. These players have developed a "hearing eye" so to speak; the ability to look at a drum part and determine from sight alone how a phrase will be articulated, swing, and ultimately sound. An individual interpretation to that phrase is then played. For starters, since drum fills are combinations of quarters, eighths, triplets, and sixteenth notes, we can use these rhythms for connecting band figures.

Let's start with a one measure ensemble rhythm from Figure Connector Study 1 from page 77 and link it by applying different subdivisions with sticking variations.

Ensemble Figure

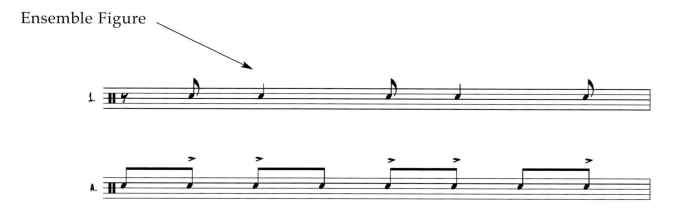

Example A uses eighth notes as the connecting rhythm as the ensemble figure is accented.

Below are examples that illustrate figure connection ideas for example 1 with:

> B. swung eighths
> C. triplets
> D. sixteenth notes

Next, experiment practicing the connector rhythms with single and double stroke sticking combinations:

1. R L R L R L R L
2. L R L R L R L R
3. R R L L R R L L
4. L L R R L L R R
5. R L R R L R L L
6. L R L L R L R R

Example B with sticking 1:

Example B with sticking 3 (RRLL):

Sticking interpretation 1 and 3 produce a different feeling to the same rhythm. Sticking 3 has a rounder more legato feel, sticking 1 is more staccato.

Below are more examples that connect ensemble figure 1 with triplets and sixteenth notes.

Example C with sticking 5 (paradiddle)

Example D combines sticking #4 (LLRR), 2 (LRLR), and 6 (LRLL)

As you can tell from the above examples, utilizing different stickings as you connect band rhythms can change the feel of a musical phrase. Horn players achieve this by using alternate fingerings for the same note. The point is to produce a con- tinuous flow of dynamics, accents, and tempo through consistent motion as you apply stickings and connecting rhythms around the instrument.

On the ensuing pages you will find several two measure band phrases that you can practice connecting. Start by playing each phrase on the snare drum, connecting each rhythm with:

   (a) Straight eighths
   (b) Swung eighths
   (c) Eighth note triplets
   (d) Sixteenth notes

For a time reference, play your hi-hat on beats 2 and 4 and the bass drum on beats 1, 2, 3, and 4 in each measure.

Once you feel comfortable with each rhythm and sticking combination. The next step is to phrase the ensemble rhythms on the drums and cymbals.

Apply the accented ensemble rhythm to:

The toms (hand to hand, right hand lead)

Connecting with eighth note double strokes starting with the left hand:

Next, try voicing the ensemble rhythm on the crash cymbal, ride, and bass drum:

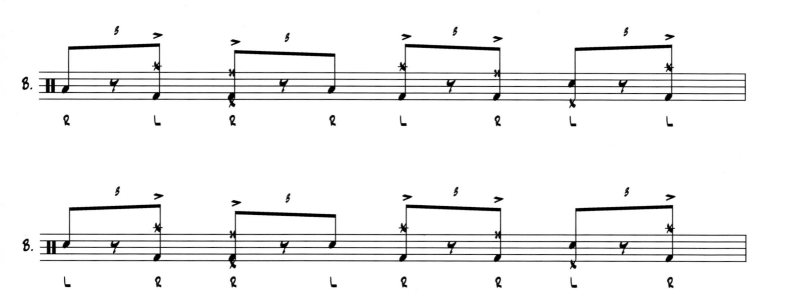

Also try combinations with the snare drum, toms, ride cymbal, crash, and bass drum:

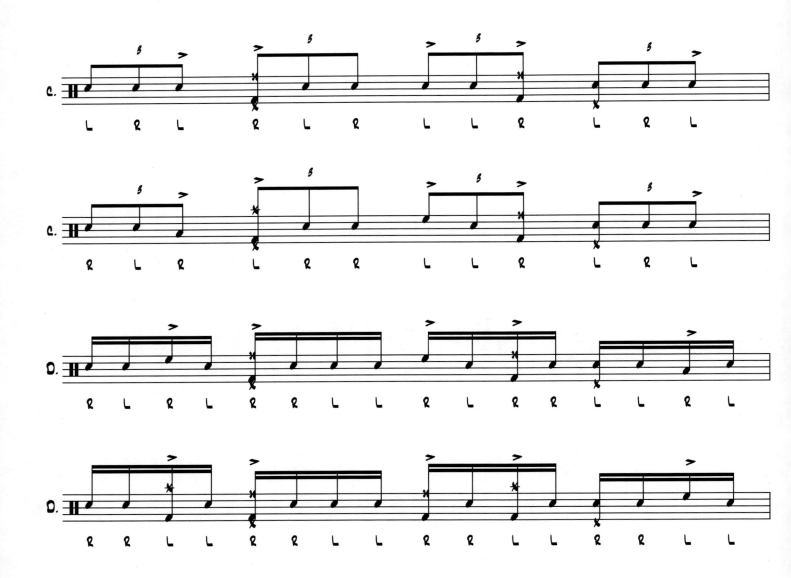

Figure Connector Study 2

Figure Connector Study in 3/4

Trumpet 1 Phrase Shapes

Below are examples extracted from the arrangements on the play along MP3 CD. Each phrase is looped or repeated several times so that you can practice it multiple times. As you experiment mirroring each phrase on the drums and cymbals, pay close attention to the articulation markings as you interpret each.

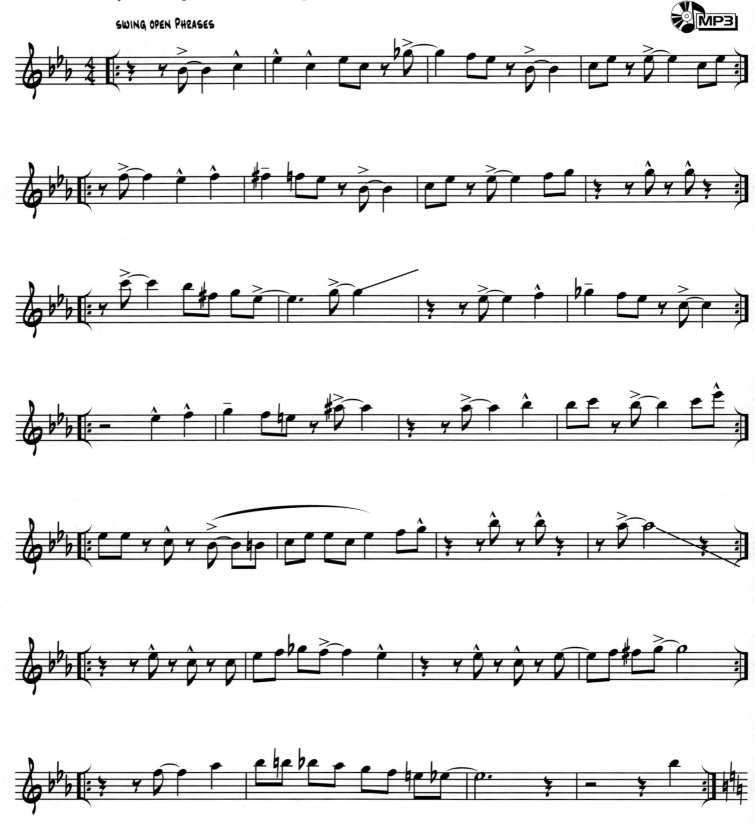

Bottom End Shuffle Phrases

Blaine Street Phrases

TIERRASANTA PHRASES

PEOPLE AND PLACES PHRASES

84

Tempo transitions move an ensemble from one time signature or musical style to another. During this change, the drummer provides rhythmic ideas that are clear and articulate, giving the band confidence and providing a smooth transition from the original tempo to the new feel.

The following examples illustrate tempo transitions in various musical styles. Stave one is how the transition would appear on a drum part, the lower stave is one approach to the transition.

In 4 Open Solos

Ballad ♩=66 Brushes

2.

JAZZ WALTZ ♩ = ♩.

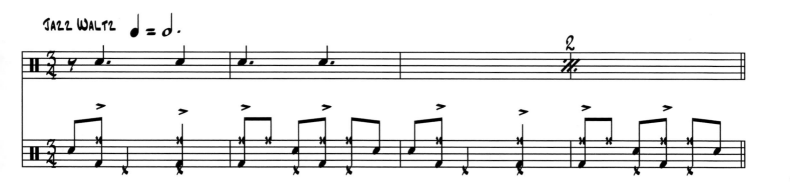

$\dot{\lrcorner} \cdot = \dot{\lrcorner}$ 12/8 FEEL

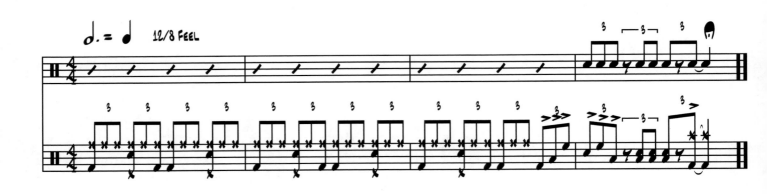

BOSSA NOVA $\dot{\lrcorner}$ = 132

3.

DOUBLE TIME SAMBA FEEL

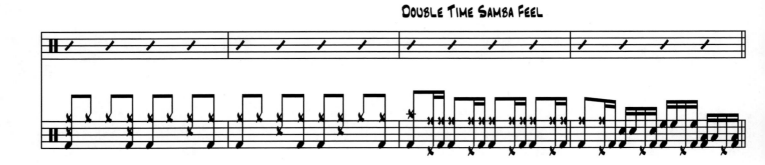

AFRO CUBAN ♩. = 126

4.

SWING ♩. = ♩

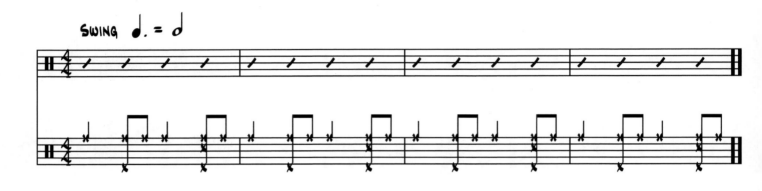

SAMBA ♩ = 132

5.

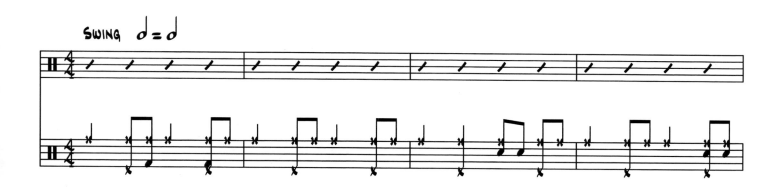

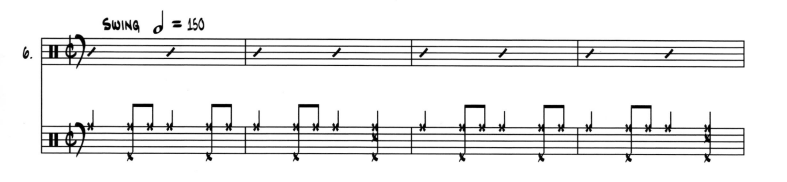

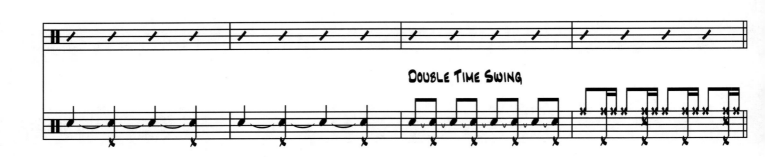

SWING IN 4

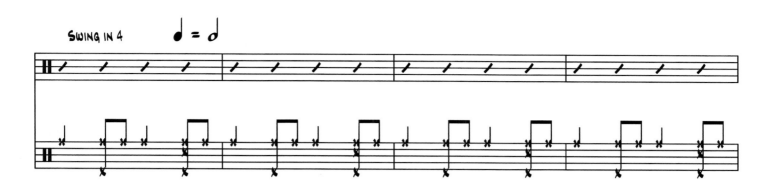

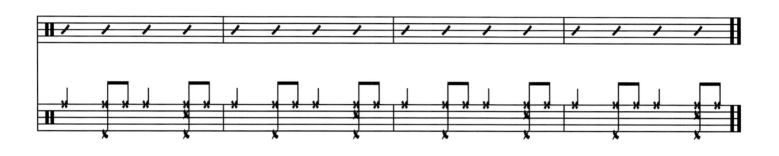

FUNKY SECOND LINE FEEL   ♩= 120

8.

SONGO ♩ = ♩

SOCA ♩ = 100

9.

94

ROCK ♩ = ♩

HALF TIME ROCK FEEL ♩ = 152

10.

Artie Shaw 1984

96

This section features five preliminary arrangements in varying styles. Practice these charts first before moving on to the band arrangements featured in the following section. Practicing an arrangement "without the band" can be a real learning experience. It forces the player to listen to his or her ideas and determine how clear they really are. Your beats, figure articulations, and set ups should "stand alone" as clear statements.

Listen to:

a. your beats and how articulate and consistent they are.
b. how the time feels and whether it is rushing or dragging as you read the part.
c. any fill set ups for clarity.
d. how you dynamically are shaping each section.

I also encourage you to record yourself playing these examples. Hearing your ideas played back on an MP3 recorder or tape player can be your best teacher in terms of what you need to work on. Focus on the things you do well and the areas that need improvement. This is the best way I know to make adjustments to any playing style.

Preliminary Chart #1

Swing ——————————————————————————————

Preliminary Chart #2

Shuffle

Ballad

Preliminary Chart #4

Samba

Funk

After a 2-bar count in, the ensemble trades two measure phrases with the drums. Establish a tight funk groove at 9. The bass enters at 19, the piano at 23. The intro is 26 measures long.

27 is the melody played by the saxophone section. As you accompany the melody, keep the intensity throughout the AAB form. Each phrase is 8 measures.

At 44, crescendo as you catch the figure at 45. Approach this figure in the same manner each time it happens: bar 261 and 269.

Play a big fill leading into the soprano sax solo at 72. Change up the feel to indicate that we are in a new part of the composition. The repeat at 76 is played 4X's.

At 104, as the soprano solo continues, transition to a strong 4 funk feel. At 121, repeat back to 104 and play both endings. Saxophone backgrounds are played the 2nd X at 114.

130, change the groove again as you accompany the bass and piano soli for 32 measures.

162 is an ensemble soli with drums. Keep a good time reference and do not play soloistically. The bass and piano are tacet. The bass enters again at 178.

193, play a big fill into 2 choruses of tenor solo at 194. At 211, repeat back to 194 and play both endings.

220 is a groove drum solo that leads into the re-statement of the melody at 236. As your solo concludes, keep the intensity and catch the figure on 4 of 235. The chart plays out from that point on.

Blaine Street
Drums

Tenor Break

Big Fill------------

194

1.

2.

212

cresc

End Tenor Solo

Blaine Street/Transcription and Justification

Blaine Street is a *feel good* funk chart that is comprised of a collection of rhythmic phrases that provide many groove opportunities. My goal with this arrangement was to form a sturdy foundation and create textural beat variations when transitioning from one phrase to another. Throughout this analysis, I present transcribed examples of melodic information with the beats I played to help illustrate the *connection* between the ensemble and drum parts.

The form of the tune is AAB with each letter representing 8 measures. Measure 44 is the only exception which is an AABB phrase. The melody begins at 27 which is the first 8 measure (A) section.

The introduction is 26 measures divided into two sections: The first, a trading phrase between the ensemble and drums, the second phrase establishes the groove and attitude of the piece at 9. The beat I came up with for the introduction is based on the rhythmic information with articulations in the trumpet and saxophone sections.

Trumpet Figure:

Saxophone Figure:

Introduction beat:

114

At 19, I transition to the ride cymbal and vary my beat slightly based on the rhythms in the bass part.

Bass part, measure 19:

Measure 19 beat:

(A) section beat at measure 27:

The bridge begins at 36 with a pedal point in the baritone sax and bass with the alto and tenor sax playing a riff motif notated below. Again, I use this information when composing.

Baritone Sax and Bass Part:

Alto and Tenor Sax Motif:

Bridge groove, bar 36:

At the end of the bridge, measures 41 through 43, there is an anticipated figure in the trombone section. I take the accented figure and incorporate it.

The phrases between measures 72 and 99 in the bass and piano parts are very static and form the groundwork for the counterpoint for the brass and reeds.

Measure 72 beat:

The two improvised solo sections are at bars 104 (soprano sax), and 194 (tenor sax). The big band is now a quartet. Below are three beat variations that I played as I accompanied both soloists:

During the brass and reed background section at bar 122 and 212, I simplify because of the number of musicians I am now accompanying:

Beginning at measure 130 is a very syncopated bass and piano soli section.

Bass and Piano measures 139-141:

To accompany this rhythmic activity, I play a distinct rhythm that is simple and easy to feel:

Following the bass and piano solo are phrases that feature the brass at 162. Again, these phrases are very syncopated and I try to use this information to compose beats that support.

The basic grooves at 162 looks like this:

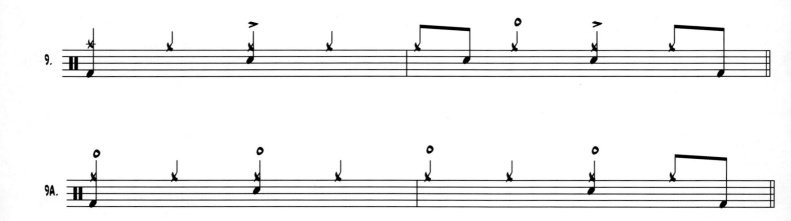

Measures 172 and 173 brass figures with drum set interpretation:

Measure 175 brass figure with drum set interpretation:

At measure 178, the brass and reeds have figures that create a 3 against 2 polyrhythm. On the following page is a transcription with two drum set interpretation examples (9D and 9E):

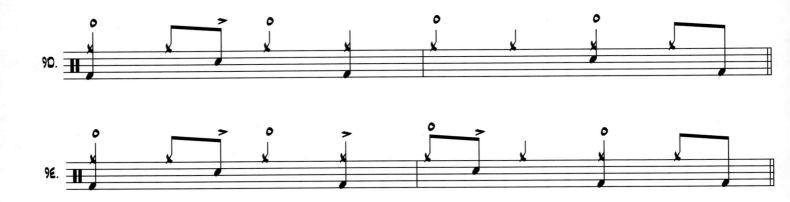

The melody is restated at measure 236, and at 284 the arrangement builds to a climax. To accommodate, I ride on my crash cymbal which creates an expansive sound.

My concept and overall musical approach for Blaine Street was inspired by the drumming of David Garibaldi of The Tower of Power band. Below are a few of my favorite recordings that I recommend that showcase his style.

The ensemble intro is 11 measures long, fortissimo dynamic. You are given a 2-measure count off into bar one. The bass trombone melody begins at 12 and is 2 choruses long. There are added brass and reed background figures at 26.

At 40, the baritone sax solo begins. On the repeat at measure 52, there are added brass background figures. As directed on the part, play the ensemble figures at 62 and 63 the last time only.

Measure 64 features 2 choruses of bass trombone and ensemble. The rhythm section is tacet.

At 86, work back into a shuffle feel and crescendo into 89 where the ensemble shout choruses run for 24 bars.

The melody returns at 113 and the chart plays out as written. Be careful not to ritard the fill in 130.

Bottom End Shuffle

Drums _____

101

113

Bottom End Shuffle/Transcription and Justification

This composition is an example of a swing shuffle. The written eighth notes are played in a swing style using this interpretation:

Bottom End Shuffle is a 12 bar blues; however, some phrases are extended and some shortened which makes reading this chart tricky the first time through it. For example, the introduction is 11 measures long and the melody is 14 measures long. The introduction is marked fortissimo and played with lots of strength and gusto. Throughout the first 6 bars of the chart, the bass trombone and baritone sax play a "pedal point" accent on beats 2 and 4. I accompany these rhythms on my floor tom and Swish Knocker cymbal. This provides a strong, deep, accent texture that mirrors the sound of the accompanying instruments.

Bass Trombone and Baritone Sax Figure   Interpretation

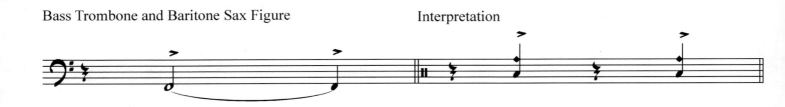

My overall approach is to make the groove feel good and not set up and "catch" many of the written figures since this can detract from the momentum of the music. The shuffle beat is dependent on the quarter note pulse for its' foundation. The snare drum usually plays the shuffle rhythm and is an essential component. When practicing with the play along MP3 CD, listen closely to the bass players' part and coordinate your limbs as you subdivide within the pulse. I recommend subdividing eighth note triplets as you hear the two measure count off into bar one. This will help you lock in the time within the opening moments of the arrangement.

My basic shuffle beat throughout looks like this:

Below are some shuffle variations for practice. You can hear these beats on the reference MP3 CD during the melody, (starting at 12), and also the baritone saxophone solo (measure 40).

At 26, I set up the brass background figures using the figure as the set up rhythm played one beat earlier on the bass drum. Throughout, I maintain the shuffle beat without disrupting the flow and feeling of the groove.

Lead Trpt Figure

Drum Set Interpretation

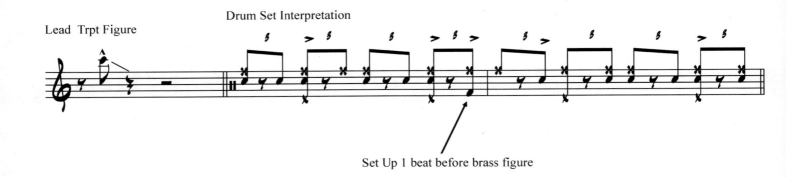

Set Up 1 beat before brass figure

Another common interpretation approach is to set up the figure on the downbeat of one.

Lead Trpt Figure

Set Up on the down beat just before the brass figure

126

Measure 40 begins the solo section featuring baritone saxophone. The "big band" is now a quartet. To accompany the baritone texture change, I transition my cymbal beat from the ride cymbal to the Swish Knocker cymbal. On the repeat at 52, the solo continues with added brass background figures. With the added horn backgrounds, the arrangement is slowly moving away from a small group texture (piano, bass, drums, and soloist).

Measure 64 features 2 choruses of bass trombone and ensemble soli without rhythm section.

At 86, I gradually work back into a shuffle and at 89 begin the ensemble shout choruses that run till measure 113. Dynamically, this is the strongest and most exciting part of the arrangement. As you listen to the reference track, notice that I set up some of the written figures, but often play the shuffle without any filling. I build the intensity and forward momentum for this section through my quarter note feel on the ride cymbal. This of course is player discretion. Feel free to try different ideas and fills and play what sounds best to you.

Measure 113 restates the melody.

Good Night Story Talk Through

This arrangement begins with an 8 measure ensemble intro. Play suspended cymbal rolls that swell and mirror the shape of the melody. Time is established at 9 with brushes.

The trombone melody enters at 9 and the song form is ABAB. Each section is 8 measures in length.

Trombone backgrounds enter at bar 23. Brass backgrounds continue and lead into the trombone solo at 41.

The last 8 bars of the trombone solo, transition from brushes to sticks and crescendo into the trombone section phrase at 59.

The trombone melody enters once again at 67. Crescendo to the dynamic high point of this arrangement at 75.

Watch the forte piano at 87 and the ritardando at 89.

Drums

49

51 TRANSITION TO STICKS

CRESC.

57 BONES

62

67 BONE MELODY

73 CRESC. ENS.

79

83 SXS. ENS.

89 RIT.

130

Good Night Story / Transcription and Justification

Good Night Story is an example of a "straight eighth" ballad that features trombone in the style of the great Stan Kenton Orchestra.

Performing ballads requires sensitivity and dynamic control that extends from pianissimo (pp) to fortissimo (ff). In many respects, brush playing is more challenging than performing with sticks because a brush will not bounce like a stick off of a drum or cymbal. Spending time practicing brush beats with recordings can help you feel confident as you begin creating beats that swing and sound balanced hand to hand. My brush concept is based on moves that my teacher Joe Morello showed me. I also listen to drummers such as Jeff Hamilton, Ed Thigpen, Shelly Manne and Philly Joe Jones and emulate what I hear. Through this experience, you will begin to understand how to accompany and paint an arrangement with the right sonic textures.

Below are some common sound conventions that you will hear on Good Night Story.

   a. suspended cymbal rolls with mallets throughout the introduction
   b. open hi-hat sound with left foot to help shade section or ensemble figures (measures 22-24, 31-32, 36-41)
   c. using the end of the push rod of the brush in the cup of the cymbal creating a bell tone or triangle effect (measures 28-29)
   d. a seamless transition to sticks at 51

Good Night Story is a 32 measure ABAB form. On the following pages are two basic brush beats I play for the melody (beat #1- measure 9 and beat #2 measure 25).

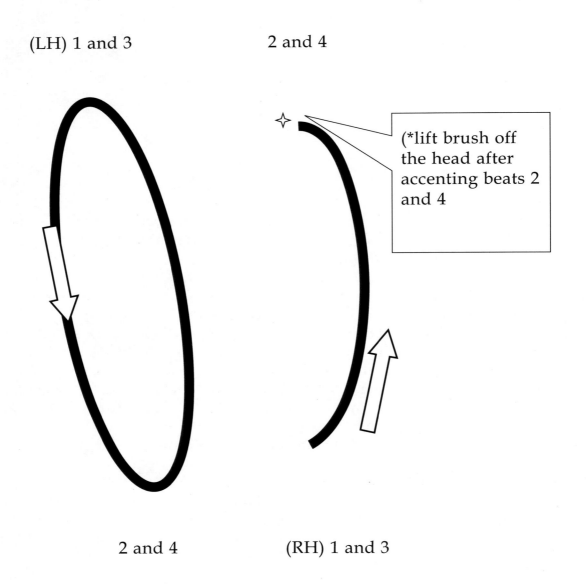

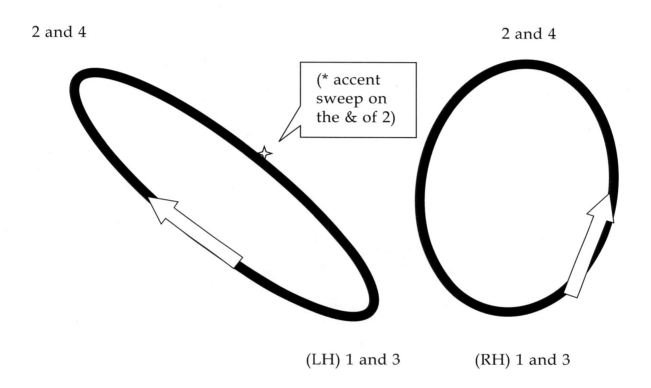

Swing Open Talk Through

After a 2 bar count-off, fill in the pick up measure leading the ensemble into their figure. The intro is 12 measures long and the melody begins at 14 and is 3 choruses. At 26, there are added trumpet background figures and at 38, added trombone figures. Throughout the melody, dynamically build intensity with each added background section.

50 features 2 choruses of soft ensemble playing commonly referred to as a soft ensemble shout. At 72 and 73, crescendo into the mezzo forte ensemble chorus at measure 74. When filling, catch the figure on 4 in 73.

Play a big fill and crescendo in 85 transitioning into the solo section at 86.

86 is repeated 9X's: 3 choruses of alto, 3 choruses of trumpet, and 3 choruses for trombone. Written backgrounds are played the last chorus of each solo.

At 98, the ensemble trades 4's with the drums for 2 choruses.

The melody returns at 122. For each of the 3 melody choruses, build intensity and crescendo into 146.

134

Drums

DRUM SOLO

DRUM SOLO

DRUM SOLO

122

FILL ----

134

Swing Open/Transcription and Justification

Swing Open is an arrangement written in the style of the great swing bands of the 1930's and 40's. The form of the composition is a blues and each section of the band contributes background riff figures as the arrangement progresses, adding intensity to the music.

To help develop the feel for this retro arrangement, listen closely to the approach of the rest of the rhythm section as they play in the classic Count Basie style with a very pronounced four feel. The bass and rhythm guitar are "laying down" a solid four with the piano mainly stating an occasional riff figure. As I composed my beats for this piece, I focused on the four feel and aimed to blend my ride cymbal beat with the quarter note rhythm that the bass and rhythm guitar were playing.

Irv Cottler

One master drummer who played great swingin' beats in this style was Irv Cottler who worked throughout the 1960's and 70's with Frank Sinatra. His beats were simply stated and always felt great. The beats on Swing Open were influenced by Irv's economical approach to time keeping.

Beat example #1 played at measure 14 in support of the saxophone section melody:

At measure 38, I change the beat texture by moving to the Swish Knocker cymbal supporting the trombone section entrance:

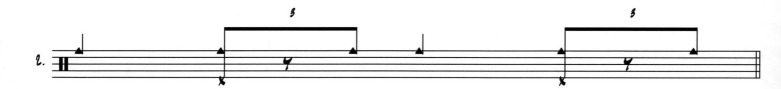

Following the ensemble and drum solo trading section at 122, I support each sections riff rhythms by playing an articulate cross stick rhythm on beats two and four on the snare drum:

As the arrangement's intensity builds, at 134 I play beat four on the snare drum (beat ex. #4), and at 146, which is the climax dynamically of this piece, I move to a back beat on beats 2 and 4 to reinforce the ensemble (beat ex. #5):

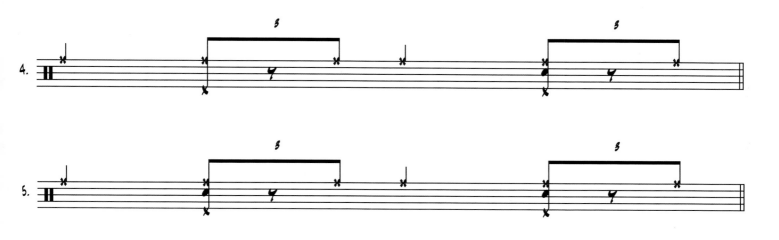

Swing Open Ensemble Phrases

On the following pages are some key ensemble phrase example transcriptions for practice. There are (3) staves of music for each. The top stave shows the drum figures as they appear on the drum part. The middle stave is the drum set transcription from the MP3 CD, and the bottom stave is the same phrase extracted from the trumpet 1 part. Having the trumpet 1 part available will also give you the most information in terms of dynamics, articulations, and phrase shape.

Phrase example #1 is the introduction to the arrangement. For the first four measures, I set up and connect the ensemble figures utilizing *parallel motion*.

Starting in measure 6, I begin creating *counter point* within the phrase using the ensemble figure as my set up fill.

parallel motion approach-setting up the band and accenting in unison

counter point approach-using the ensemble figure as my set up rhythm

142

Phrase example #2 begins at measure 50 and continues through bar 61. The overall phrasing approach throughout this example is *parallel*. I maintain the flow during the phrase by continuing to play time on the ride cymbal.

Example #3 begins at measure 62 and like the previous phrase, the approach utilized is parallel. In measure four while the band is resting, I *connect* the end of bar three to measure five by voicing eighth notes on the drums and Swish Knocker cymbal.

144

Example #4 starts at measure 74. Again, the approach utilized is parallel. During the alto saxophone solo break in bars 84 and 85, I set up the quarter note ensemble figure on beat four of measure 85 using a simple connector rhythm on the snare drum and floor tom.

Tierrasanta Talk Through

This arrangement begins with a 26 measure ensemble intro. Establish a samba feel at 27. At 35, the melody enters. The song form is AABA with a 16 measure bridge. The A sections are 8 measures each.

75 is the ensemble soli. At the bridge, bar 91, return to the samba groove.

The trombone solo begins at 117. Play down through 172 and repeat back to 133. Backgrounds are played 2nd X only.

At 173, the ensemble trades 4's with the drums and solo around the horn figures through 204.

Bars 205-221 decrescendo into the start of the alto solo. The solo continues to measure 266, then repeat back to measure 230. The backgrounds are played 2nd X only.

Drums are out at 266.

The melody returns at 282 and at 324, piano and bass are tacet. At 340, the entire rhythm section is in for the remainder of the chart.

148

149

151

153

Tierrasanta is a fast Brazilian arrangement. The musical style marked on the drum chart maintains that it is a Samba; however, the rhythmic information played by the rhythm section and horns define it as a Baiao. The beat I came up with centers around this foundational rhythm played by the electric bass.

Baiao bass line:

In addition to the Baiao rhythm, I incorporate the melodic information beginning at measure 35 played by the alto, trombone, and trumpet.

(A) section beat at measure 35:

The hand pattern between the bell of the ride cymbal and snare drum is a paradiddle, one of the standard 26 drum rudiments. This groove, when layered over top of the melody, creates a syncopated feel that helps support the melody. I also play this beat during the trombone solo at bar 133, and again at measure 282 where the melody is restated.

The melody begins at measure 35 and the form of the tune is AABA. Each (A) section is 8 measures long, and the (B) section is 16 bars.

The beat for the 16 measure bridge section at measure 51 incorporates the rhythms played by the saxophone section. Since the music has transitioned to a different part of the form, I vary the groove to match the dynamic of the phrase. At this juncture, the electric bass rhythm also changes and plays a standard Samba bass line.

154

Saxophone section motif at measure 51.

The bell of the ride cymbal coupled with the cross stick on the snare drum gives the band clear, articulate sounds that will make for clean section entrances across the ensemble.

Bridge groove, measure 51:

The third groove that makes up this arrangement begins at 75. The drum chart informs us to play a dry feel. So everyone can hear and feel the pulse clearly, I voice eighth notes on the hi-hat, accenting the Samba rhythm. Below is the melodic information that led me to this choice.

Trumpet 1, measure 75:

Bass and bass trombone information, measures 77 through 79:

155

Measure 75 beat:

Bar 173 begins a "trading 4's" section between the ensemble and drums. This is followed by the section at 205 marked gradual decrescendo. To accompany this, I play the same beat as I did at 75, and continue it throughout the first two (A) sections of the alto solo at 222. This groove can also be heard again at measure 324.

This arrangement begins with a free open drum solo. As you develop your ideas, disregard the reference click track, horn chorale cues, and fermatas. At 10, establish a fast swing feel. At 18, the drum solo ends and time is firmly established.

Crescendo leading into the melodic theme at 26. Shape the start of the theme the same way each time it happens: 62, 94, 224, and 306.

The song form is AABA with each phrase being 8 measures long (1 chorus ='s 32 bars).

At 39, dynamically taper your fill down into the guitar solo at 42.

78 through 93 is a saxophone and trombone soli and bar 94 is a re-statement of the ensemble theme.

112 is stop time. Be careful and subdivide throughout this section so that the figures are accurately played. The stop time sets up 3 choruses of trombone solo starting at 128. Brass backgrounds are played on the third chorus.

The trombone solo ends at 224. At 239, D.S. back to measure 128 for 3 choruses of tenor solo with backgrounds last X. Play down through 207, and jump to the coda in measure 240.

256, the tenor sax solo winds down to a piano, bass, and drums vamp.

Saxophones enter at 264. Carefully count at 280 since this is a 10 bar phrase. The trombones enter at 290. 297, the entire ensemble is in.

349, the arrangement begins winding down and at 366, when the trumpet section enters, crescendo into 370 and play the chart out fortissimo.

People and Places
Drums

Composed and Arranged by Ryan Haines

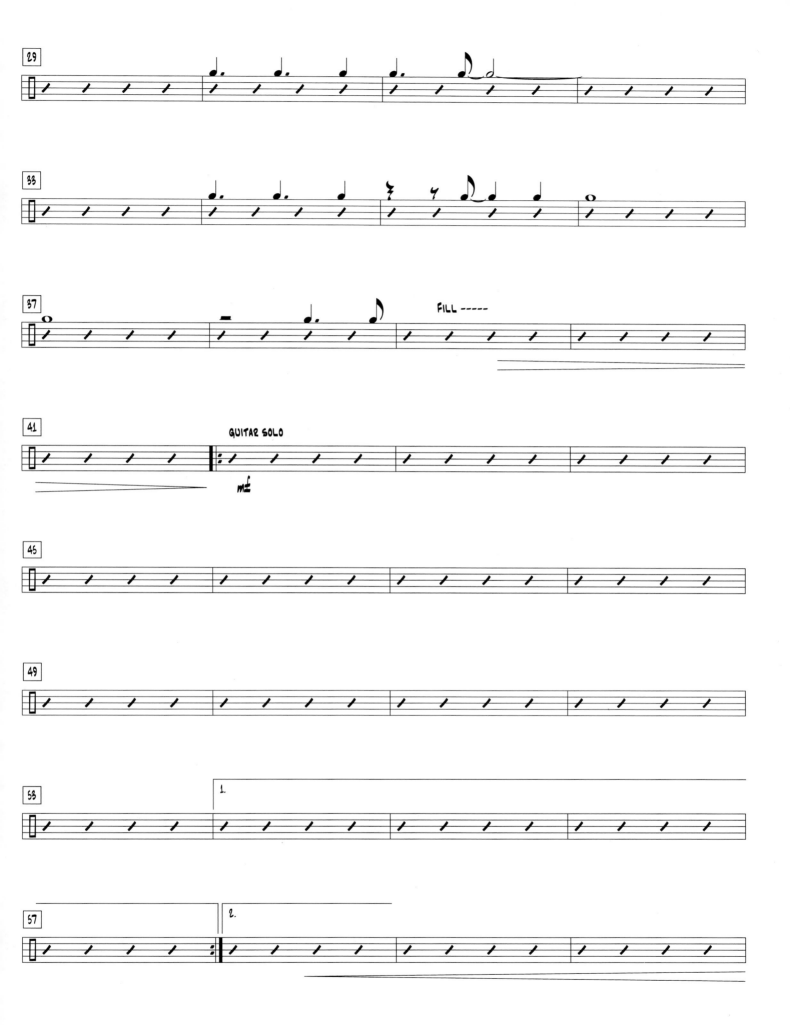

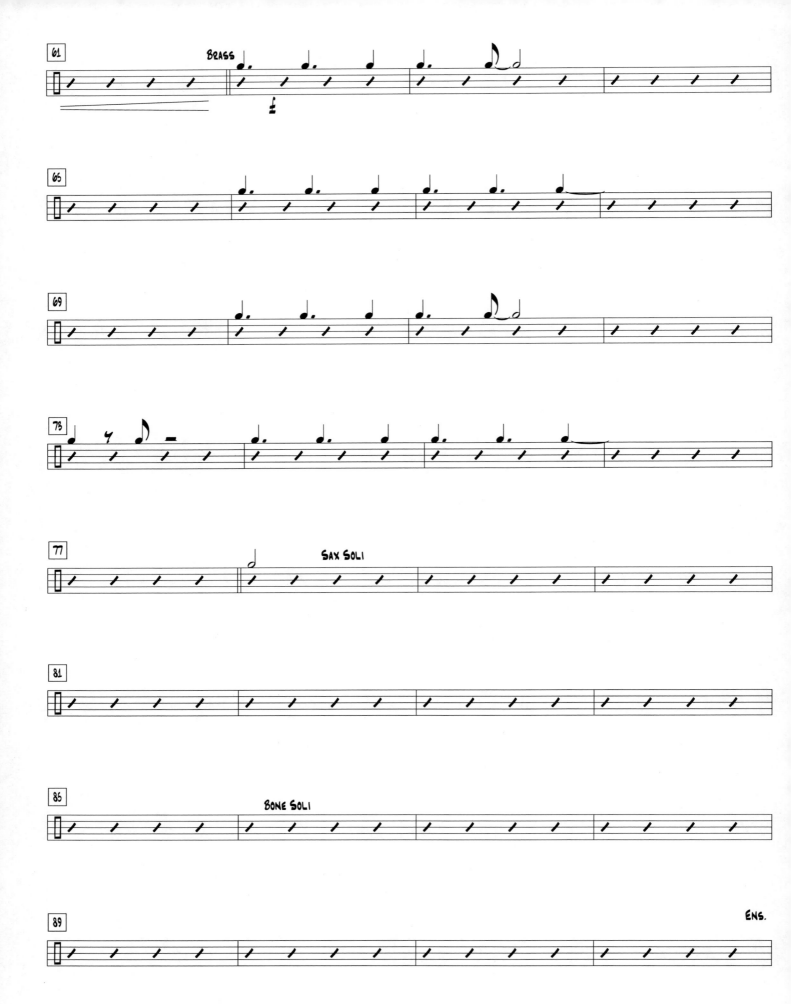

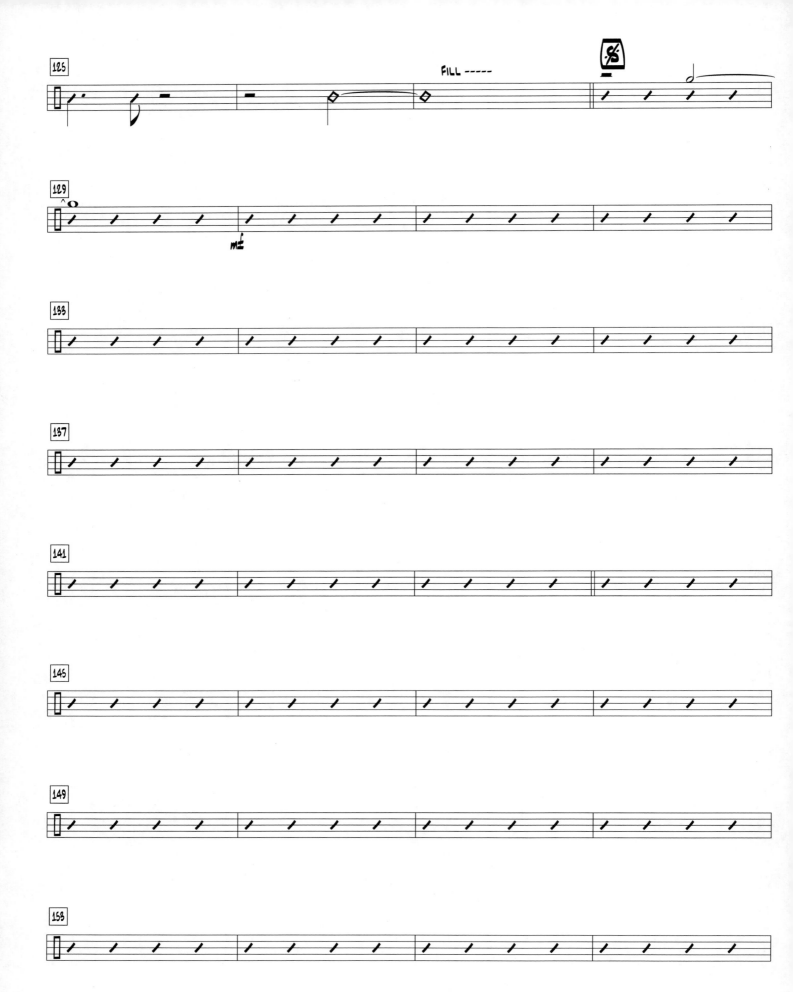

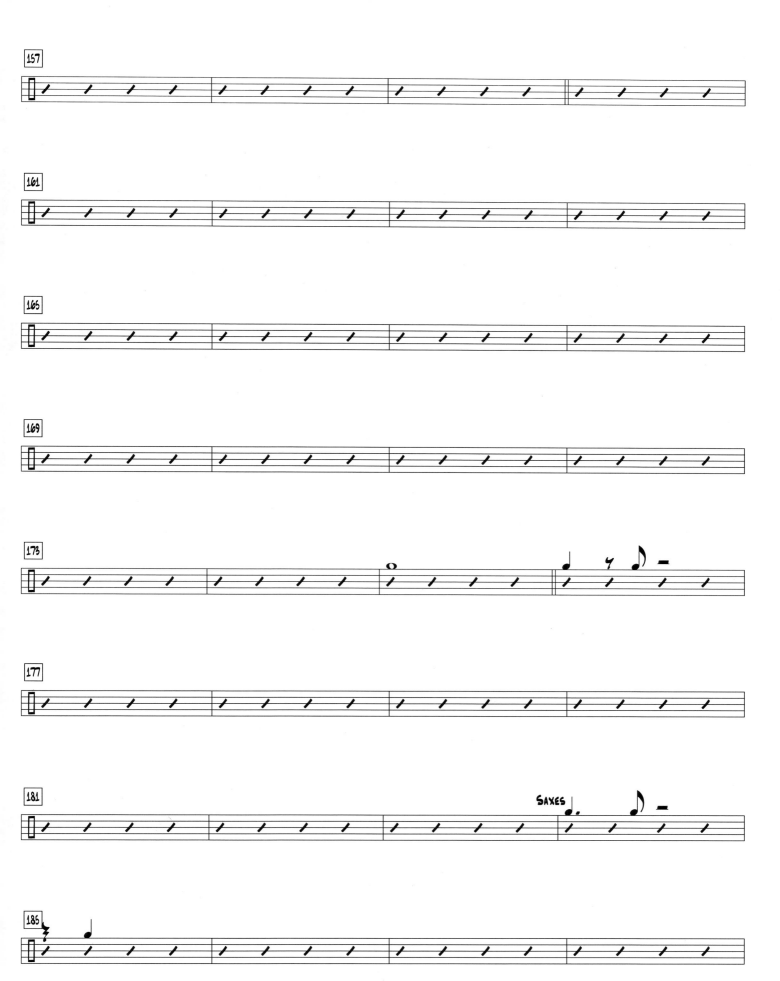

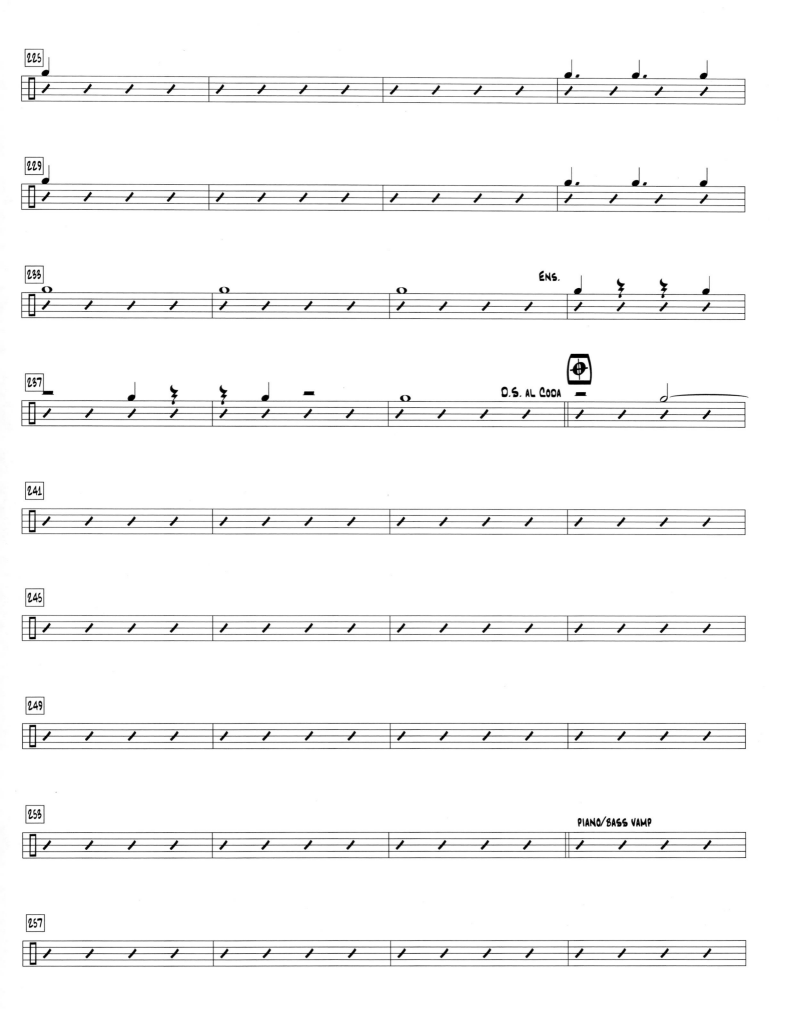

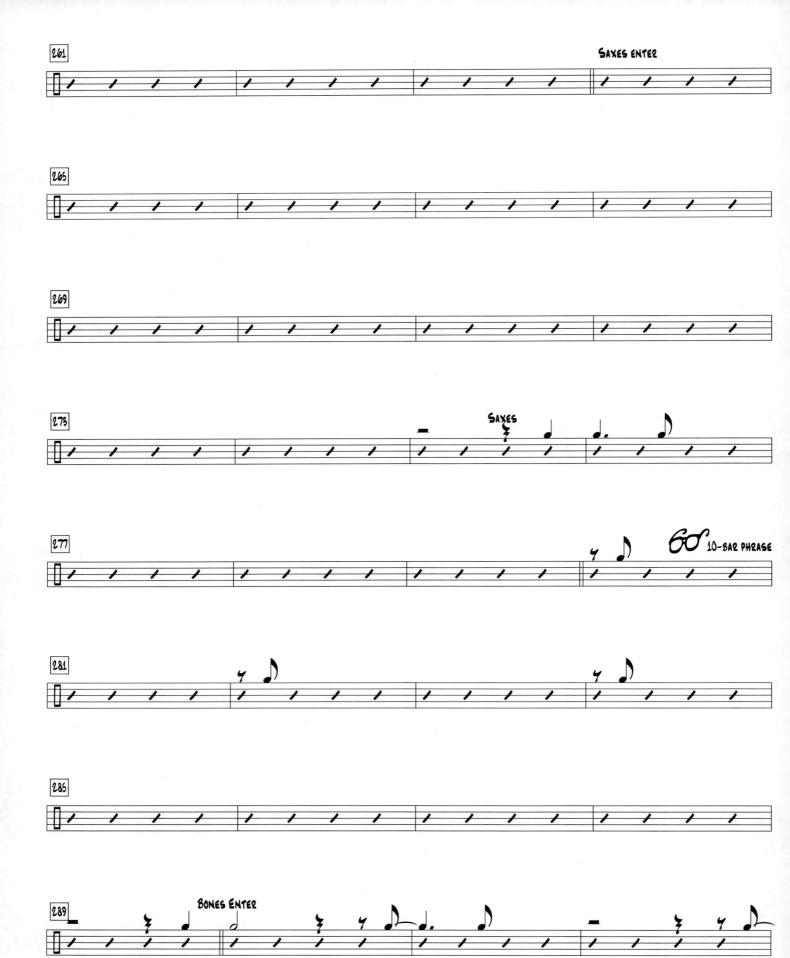

People and Places/Transcription and Justification

People and Places is an example of an up tempo swing chart. My favorite band to gain inspiration from regarding this style is Woody Herman's Swingin' Herd from 1963. This ensemble featured the great drumming of Jake Hanna. The amazing thing about Jake's playing is that he could groove on tempos of 400 beats per minute AND faster for very long periods of time and still remain relaxed!!!!

The challenge with playing fast tempos is keeping your mind and body relaxed so that the flow of the time is not disrupted. Breathing deeply and *thinking* longer phrases as you play can help. When I play fast tempos, I count and subdivide by the measure, or sometimes every two measures. This helps my beats feel looser and more comfortable.

For example, instead of counting each beat in the measure when playing your swing pattern,

try counting each measure by breathing in deeply for one bar and exhaling in the second measure.

If the tempo is extremely fast (300 beats per minute and faster), I think and count every two measures, breathing in for two and out for two.

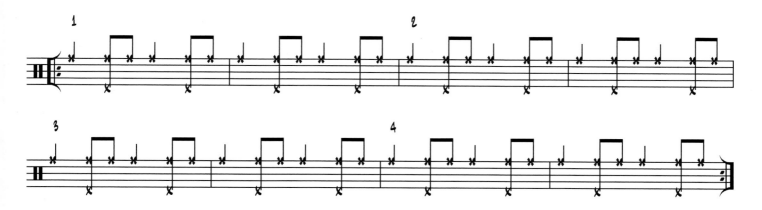

These counting techniques help me feel less restrictive about playing fast and enable me to play for longer periods of time.

Another common technique to help with relaxation when playing fast is to alter the phrasing of your ride cymbal beat. The following page illustrates a few ways I phrased the cymbal beat on the reference MP3 CD.

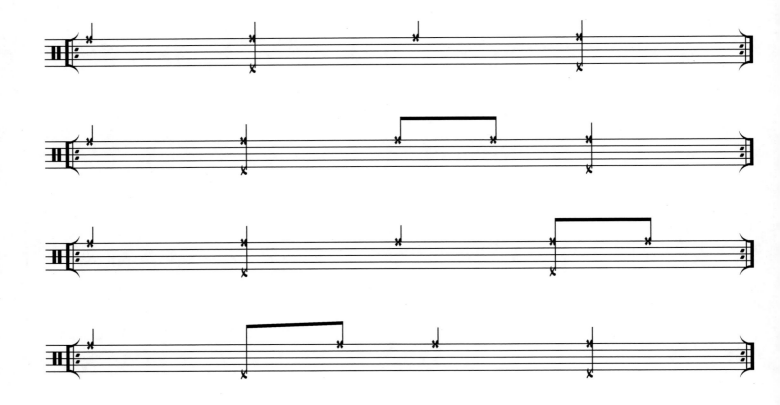

Looking at the drum part for "People and Places," the introduction is an open drum solo with horn chorale cues. On the MP3 CD, you will hear a click track reference at a half note of 140 beats per minute throughout the drum solo introduction. When we originally record-ed this for Ryan Haines, this section was done as a separate piece that needed to be "fitted" to the new tempo established at 18. When I soloed, I disregarded the click and played ideas that were free with no tempo reference. The only solo suggestion I was given at the time was to play a closed roll at the beginning and develop into other ideas from that. I came out of my solo and established tempo at 14.

This is a fun arrangement to play because of the amount of freedom given to each soloist. At 42 begins a guitar solo and at 78 a sax soli, followed by a trombone soli at 86. At 112 there is a trombone solo with stop time and on the D.S. back to 128, features a tenor sax solo. For each, the rhythm section fluctuates between a broken/float feel and eventually builds into a driving 4 feeling. If you decide to approach the solo sections like this, count carefully as you break up your ideas because when you perform with a live band, you may run the risk of losing some of your band mates if they're having trouble feeling the pulse.

The lead trumpet figure is the main ensemble motif throughout the piece.

It is used to transition the arrangement from one section to the next. I interpret this phrase using a parallel approach voicing each on a long sustained sound because this is the approach the lead trumpet player uses. You will hear me perform that phrase on combinations of crash cymbal and bass drum as well as snare drum and crash cymbal. As I move with the ensemble and connect the rhythm, I play it with the same amount of intensity. I'm also dynamically leading the ensemble into the figure with a crescendo beginning a minimum of four measures before the ensemble entrance which allows for a smooth dynamic transition.

Solos and Transcriptions

Gene Krupa and Buddy Rich

Drum solos can fluctuate in duration ranging from a few beats or measures to extended statements, utilizing various solo formats such as trading 4's or 8's, to an open solo. They can be in time, following the form of the song (12 measure blues form or 32 bar song form), or they can be free of form without any feeling of time or tempo.

The "drum solo" was brought to the forefront by the first wave of big band drummers. Chick Webb, Gene Krupa, and Buddy Rich were marvelous soloists and helped standardize the open drum solo format. This type of solo was designed to feature the drummers' technical abilities as well as his showmanship. Most drum solos from the big band era were free,

meaning the drummer played until the ensemble was cued back into the arrangement. Great solos are improvisational, and as drummers, we have many sounds on our instrument that create texture and shape. Today we still listen and gain inspiration from drum solos that were played over fifty years ago because they are logical, musical, and technical, which in turn makes them interesting. Try approaching your solo as if you are telling a story, the beginning is where the major themes are introduced and the middle is where they are developed. The end can repeat ideas that you already played or finish with a new statement.

Dynamics and orchestration

The use of dynamics when soloing can create contrast, mood, and interest. A drum solo performed at one dynamic level will generate a monotone quality that is not very interesting or musical. Changes in dynamics make solo statements more engaging for the listener.

Orchestration is the development of single rhythmic ideas played on your toms, snare, bass, and cymbals producing tonal effects. Orchestrating rhythmic phrases and the use of dynamics and textures will produce variation in your solo statements.

The following pages contain transcription examples of ensemble set up fills from some of the greatest bands, drummers, and recordings from the big band idiom. Also included are two open solo examples and one call and response solo. These transcriptions trace the development and lineage of the modern drum solo.

The first example is *Sing Sing Sing* from Gene Krupa with Benny Goodman from the 1938 recording *Live at Carnegie Hall*. This solo is built on ideas that repeat helping the ensemble and soloists transition from one segment of the arrangement to the next. This solo showcases Gene Krupa's style beautifully and was an innovation that helped bring the drums from being solely an accompaniment instrument to an equal musical member of the band.

As you practice this transcription, focus on:

- the bass drum consistency throughout each solo statement which adds forward momentum to his ideas.
- wide dynamic range as he creates a jungle effect texture on the floor tom.
- the outstanding authority and confidence throughout entire solo.
- the use of accents creating a second tier of swing.

SING SING SING - Solo Transcription

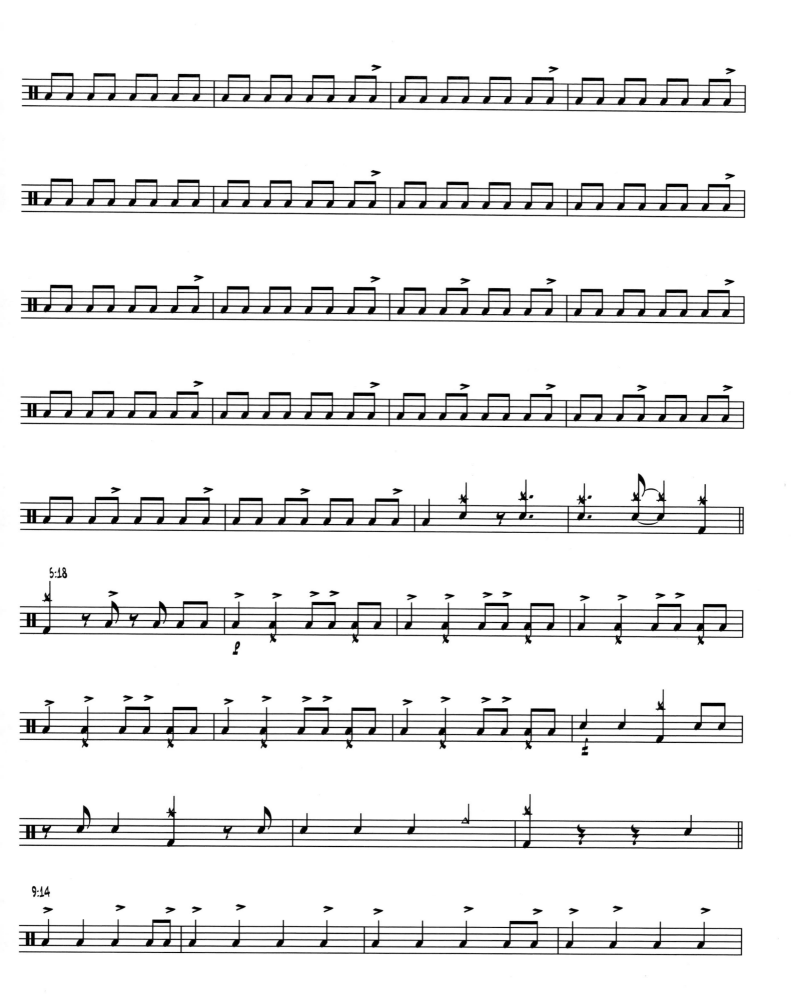

DESCRESC.

11:35

drum solos begins at 1:29. These solos are innovative because they document the first time double bass drums were used as a solo device on record. Also, Louie wrote and arranged this composition for Duke Ellington's Orchestra which was an innovation all its own.

As you practice this transcription, focus on:

- brilliant technical control and flexibility around the drum set.
- the bass drum is used consistently at times playing quarter notes adding drive to the phrases. He also substitutes rhythms on the bass drums that would normally be played with his hands.
- most long phrases begin with combinations of snare and bass drum patterns.
- Louie's *legato* touch which is very difficult to produce at these tempos.

The second example is *Skin Deep* from Louie Bellson with Duke Ellington from the 1951 recording, *Ellington Uptown*. The first eight bar break occurs at 1:05 on the track and serves as a transitional solo from the medium tempo to the break neck tempo of half note equaling 208 beats per minute! It's remarkable to imagine soloing over this tempo; however, Louie does it with ease. The first of two extended

LOUIE BELLSON

179

SKIN DEEP - Solo Transcription 1

BD SIMILE

SKIN DEEP - Solo Transcription 2

DECRESC

DOUBLE BASS DRUM SIMILE

185

Double Bass Drum Simile throughout

187

TACIT BD

DOUBLE BASS DRUM SIMILE

188

The last example is the *West Side Story Medley* from Buddy Rich from the recording *Swingin' New Big Band Live at the Chez*. This is arguably the finest recorded example of Buddy Rich ever. His swing feel is light and deep and his solo ideas are simply remarkable. The extended solo begins at 8:55.

As you practice this transcription, focus on:

- Buddy's ideas are centered on the snare drum with all patterns played as single strokes.
- The bass drum is used significantly as a third hand.
- phrases that resolve on the crash cymbal or by crashing the shoulder of the ride cymbal.
- his extraordinary command and control of his ideas and time feel throughout.

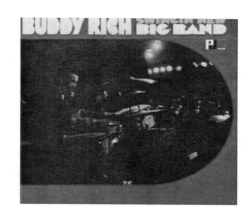

Behind Buddy's Slingerland drumset at the Zildjian Factory in Norwell, Massachusetts

BD SIMILE

191

Drum Solo Breaks

Ensemble Shout Chorus Transcription Excerpts

♩ = 68

JEEP'S BLUES (INTRODUCTION), DUKE ELLINGTON ORCHESTRA, ELLINGTON AT NEWPORT, SAM WOODYARD

HALF OPEN HIGH HAT

♩ = 236

OPUS ONE (2:33), TERRY GIBBS DREAM BAND VOL. 1, MEL LEWIS

♩ = 138

SHINY STOCKINGS (3:40), COUNT BASIE ORCHESTRA, LIVE AT THE SANDS, SONNY PAYNE

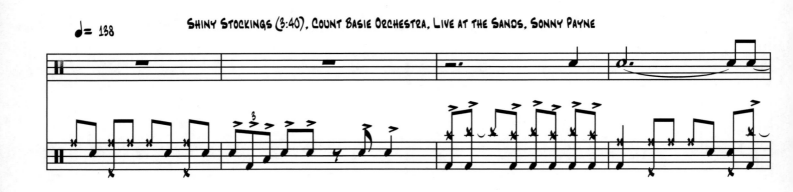

♩= 116 BASICALLY BLUES (1:17), BUDDY RICH BIG BAND, SWINGIN NEW BIG BAND

♩= 136 A LITTLE MINOR BOOZE (5:11), STAN KENTON ORCHESTRA, LIVE AT REDLANDS UNIVERSITY, JOHN VON OHLEN

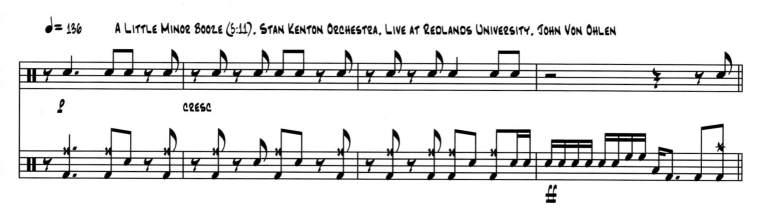

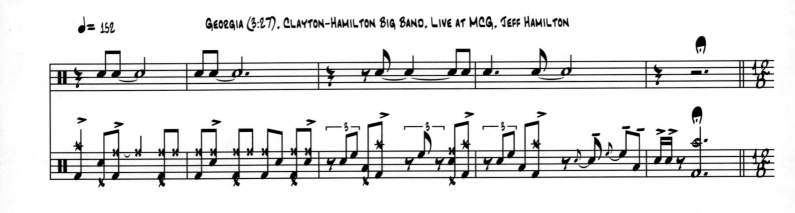

Georgia (3:27), Clayton-Hamilton Big Band, Live at MCG, Jeff Hamilton

Make Someone Happy (3:01), Woody Herman Swingin' Herd, Woody Live East and West, Ronnie Zito

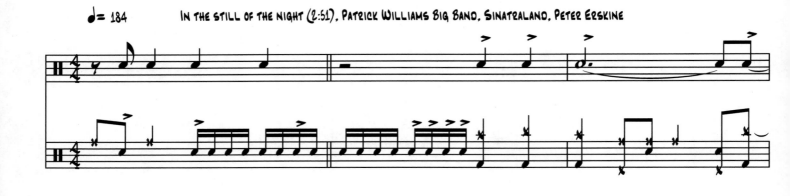

In the still of the night (2:51), Patrick Williams Big Band, Sinatraland, Peter Erskine

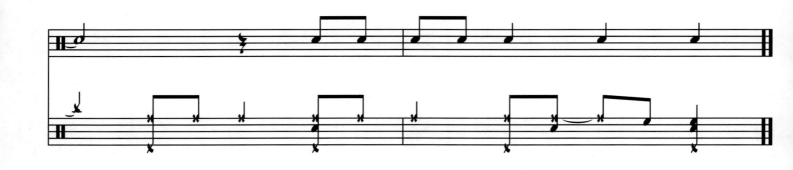

Big Band Drumming Innovators and Innovations

Throughout the early part of the twentieth century, players like Baby Dodds, Zutty Singleton, and Paul Barbarin refined the discoveries of parade and brass band drummers of New Orleans by applying their march rhythms to a new instrument: A con-trap-tion we know today as the drum set. In addition to codifying the discoveries of early march drummers, they added significant musical contributions of their own.

The 1930s saw major changes in America and the music business. Due to the stock market crash of 1929, America's economy was non-existent. Slowly, the country's situation began to improve with the help of music and its main medium, radio.

Because swing music was so popular and financially lucrative, ballrooms, clubs, theatres, and hotels welcomed orchestras. Bands like Benny Goodman, Duke Ellington, Artie Shaw, Tommy Dorsey, Chick Webb, Jimmie Lunceford, and Glenn Miller helped Americans forget their financial troubles and hoist the country from the Great Depression. These orchestras could be heard on radio remote broadcasts from hotel ballrooms across the United States.

The big band drummers of the 1930s and 40s such as Chick Webb, Gene Krupa, Dave Tough, Jo Jones, Ray McKinley, and Buddy Rich helped influence the style of the first wave of be bop drummers such as Kenny Clarke, Max Roach, Art Blakey, and Stan Levy. These forward thinkers helped modernize drumming. Their innovations paralleled experimentation within jazz. Because of these players and countless others, the drummer's role became increasingly more important. Each drumming generation slowly assumed more responsibility in the jazz band.

Hank Levy

Chick Webb 1938

The following interview is with drummer Eddie Jenkins who replaced Buddy Rich with Bunny Berigans' Band in 1939. Frequently Jenkins went "uptown" to hear Chick Webb at the Savoy Ballroom in Harlem and they became friends.

My first exposure to Chick Webb was like lightning striking.....BOOM! A high school friend from White Plains, NY took me to the Savoy Ballroom for the first time to hear the battle of the bands. In those days, the bands at the hotels would play their gig, and then play a set at the Savoy, the Brooklyn Roseland, and then the Broadway Roseland. They made that circuit and then went back to their regular gigs. That particular night, there was a benefit at the Savoy for the American Federation of Musicians. Glen Gray's Casa Loma Orchestra was there that night, Benny Goodman's Orchestra, The Savoy Sultans, Chick Webb....all the bands that worked theaters and hotels were there. Out on the street, people were congregating to get into the Savoy and Chick Webb was standing outside selling tickets for the benefit! He sold me mine! I didn't know Chick Webb from Adam. After that night, I began making trips to the Savoy on Tuesday nights to hear Chick.

Eddie Jenkins also discussed the first time he sat in with the Chick Webb Orchestra:

It was customary for one of the trumpet players from the section to play drums during the first set when Chick wouldn't show up. Beverly Peer was Chick's bass player, and when I stood near the bandstand to see Chick, Peer was positioned nearest to me and we became friends. Through my meetings with Beverly and the trumpet players on the band, one night one of them asked me If I would like to sit in for Chick since he was run-

ning late....so that's how that came about. The band didn't play any wild stomping stuff. We played for the dancers and it was a wonderful experience.

Chick Webb's style fused rudimental, military drumming with swing. He was the first to bring the drums to the fore front of jazz through his technical solos, dynamic control, and imaginative breaks and fills. Although he was unable to read music, he committed to memory the arrangements played by the band and directed performances from a raised platform in the center of the ensemble.

His set was built specifically for him by the Gretsh-Gladstone Drum Company. It was a console set up that included a rail that was attached to a 28" bass drum. It was built on wheels which made it easier to position and move off stage. The rail had a table attached that held all of Chick's accessories: temple blocks, cowbells, sticks, brushes, and mallets. Unlike other drummers of the 1920's, he used the wood blocks and cowbells only for momentary effects, and varied his playing with rim shots, temple block work, and cym-

With Eddie Jenkins of Arlington Virginia, March 2007

bal crashes. In addition to the table, bass drum and rail system, he used a snare drum with wooden rims, a 9X13 inch tom tom mounted to the rail on the bass drum, and a 16X16 inch floor tom. His Zildjian cymbals (2) were suspended by straps on gooseneck stands also attached to the console rail. His larger cymbal was on the right, the smaller of the two on the left. Both cymbals were less than 18" in diameter. On his far right, he used a large Chinese cymbal. His hi-hat cymbals were no larger than 12 inches. The standard hi-hat sizes of the 1930's were 10 or 11 inches.

There are many excellent examples of Webb's drumming on record to study, analyze, and learn from. One of his most popular is *Spinnin' the Webb, the Original Decca Recordings.*

All transcriptions included throughout this section use the following eighth note interpretation:

$$\eighthnotes = \text{triplet}$$

To hear a sample of his solo style, listen to *Harlem Congo* and *Liza*. Both depict Chick's complete command and technical control of the drum set.

On *Don't Be That Way*, we hear a very early approach to playing ensemble figures during a shout chorus. Chick creates rhythmic counterpoint by playing or "pushing" the same rhythm one beat before the band plays. This "push beat" happens on the last two bars of the first (A) section of the shout chorus.

Push Beat Transcription Example from Don't Be That Way - Chick Webb

The bridge section features an eight measure drum solo where he incorporates eighths, triplets, and sixteenth note phrasing producing a looser feel that resembles ideas that Jo Jones played with the Count Basie Band a decade later. This affect is achieved in part by the absence of the bass drum playing four quarter note beats to the bar which is at the center of every Webb performance.

On the track, *Clap Hands Here Comes Charlie*, Webb displays his sensitivity for supporting a soloist by constantly changing sounds during the accompaniment. On the (A) sections of the tenor solo for example, he plays the hi-hat in a traditional manner, but on the bridge when the clarinet enters, he plays the hi-hat closed at a soft dynamic. During the piano solo, he changes the texture by moving to the console rail to play time. His drum breaks leading into the last chorus are played on wood blocks and cowbell to add variety and color.

Dave Tough- The Subtle Swinger

Dave Tough was known for his subtly. His beat was strong and intense, but not heavy handed. He played with a light touch on the drums and cymbals, and unlike most drummers, he disliked performing drum solos. From listening to recordings and reading interviews, his main objective was to create texture and color through the drum set as he accompanied arrangements and soloists. These attributes were his innovations to drumming, and more importantly music. Drummers who followed in his musical wake were Mel Lewis, Joe Morello, and Jeff Hamilton.

Dave Tough was born in 1908 and raised in Oak Park, Illinois and is usually linked with Dixieland jazz. Many consider him a transi-

Dave Tough testing cymbals at the Avedis Zildjian factory in Quincy, Massachusetts

204

tional drummer who was versatile enough to play Dixieland and the new be-bop style of the late 1940's. He played with Tommy Dorsey's Big Band throughout 1936 and 37 and replaced Gene Krupa with Benny Goodman for a four month span in 1938. He returned to Tommy Dorsey in the summer of 1939.

Tough also served in the Artie Shaw Navy Band from 1942-44 and from 1944-45. He made a dominant impact as drummer with Woody Herman's First Herd.

His drum and cymbal set up was consistent throughout his career. He used a 24" or 26" bass drum and a 14" snare drum. His two small toms mounted on the bass drum replaced the trap table/temple block set up that was popular at that time. His floor tom size was 16" and he kept all his drums tuned fairly low. His hi-hats were 10" or 11" and a little heavier than paper thin. He used a series of small crash cymbals, medium heavy in weight, mounted on the bass drum or on stands. His Chinese cymbal had rivets to enhance the sound, and was kept to his right and used for backing shout choruses or out choruses of arrangements.

Dave Tough popularized the sound of the Chinese cymbal more so than any other drummer. Cozy Cole also used one, as did Jimmy Crawford with Jimmy Lunceford's band. The Chinese cymbal produces a driving sound and because it is low in pitch, it complements instruments or ensemble passages without being too direct.

Tough was also a well read, knowledgeable intellect. In 1937 he wrote a column for Metronome Magazine entitled *Hide Hitters Hangout* where he took questions from readers and followed up with answers. Topics included: tuning, equipment choice, rudiments, and practice suggestions.

Dave Tough with the Artie Shaw Navy Band, 1944

Below is an excerpt from Dave's metronome column from June 1937 providing counsel to a reader who is having issues with hi-hat cymbals.

Mr. J.O.B., of Middletown, Conn., writes in and asks what size and type cymbals should be used on a high–hat. He also wants to know if the cymbals should be fully released at the top of the beat.

In the first place throw away the cymbals that come with the thing, and buy the best ones you can get your hands on. Ten or eleven inch Zildjian cymbals, both the same size and just a little heavier than paper thin, give good results. You can get a smoother swing if you keep the cymbals touching each other all the time. Raising your foot high and releasing them completely throws the accent too definitely on the beat, and tends to make the rhythm clumsy.

DAVE

To gain an understanding of his playing style, a collection of recordings by Woody Herman's First Herd consisting of rehearsals from 1944 for the Old Gold Cigarette radio show are excellent examples. These rehearsals were primarily organized to check broadcast times and microphone levels. You can hear Dave Tough's drum and cymbal sounds with remarkable quality and clarity on these recordings.

For a sample of his accompaniment style, check out *Is You Is or Is You Ain't My Baby*. This is a perfect example of changing sounds and textures behind different sections of an arrangement.

Dave's beat is loose, light, and phrased with an emphasis on the triplet subdivision.

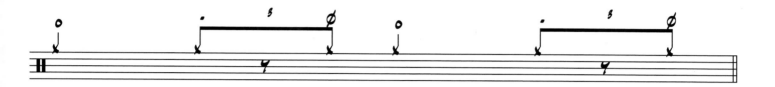

For the introduction to this arrangement he plays the hi-hat cymbals with great strength, using the cymbals to support the ensemble and catch accents.

Is You Is or Is You Ain't (My Baby) introduction transcription- Dave Tough

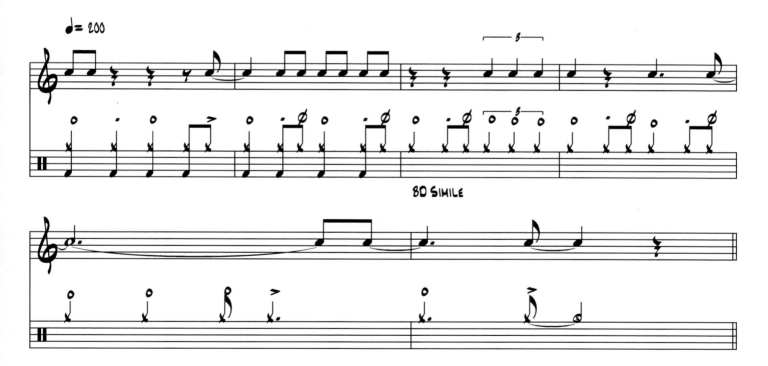

The form of this tune is AABA, with each lettered section equaling 8 measures. For the vocal melody, Dave changes with the form. For the A sections, he plays on the closed hi-hat and makes accents on the hi-hat stand with his left stick. The ringing that you hear is the stand itself.

To mark the B section, he changes his hi-hat pattern by opening and closing the cymbals.

For each soloist he accompanies, he uses different cymbals to support each soloist. For the tenor solo, he plays time on the Chinese cymbal, and then moves to the traditional open and closed hi-hat sound for the trumpet and trombone solos. For the softer dynamic of the clarinet solo, he plays time on the closed hi-hat.

Is You Is or Is You Ain't (My Baby) time playing transcription accompanying the tenor solo - Dave Tough

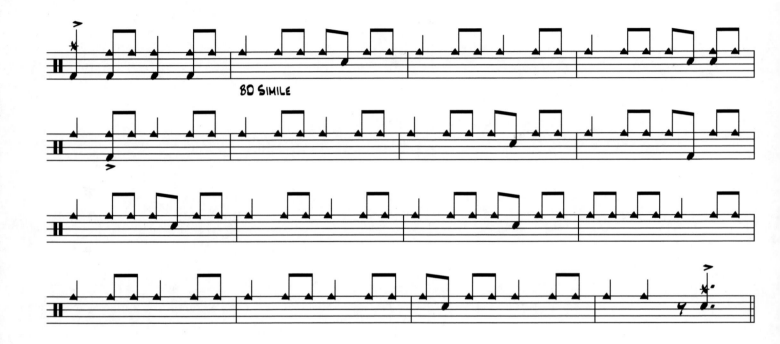

Gene Krupa, circa 1940

Gene Krupa combined the technical big band style of Chick Webb with the New Orleans parade band tradition developed by Baby Dodds. He was born in Chicago in 1909 and as a teenager befriended several young Chicago jazz men including Bud Freeman, Eddie Condon, and Jimmy McPartland. These men helped develop the Chicago Jazz Style of the 1920's by moving away from a two beat feel and into four beat swing. For an example of Gene's early work, check out "China Girl" from the Okeh session of 1927. The band's swing feel resonates from the bass drum as he plays 4/4 throughout the track. This was an innovation because it was the first time a bass drum was documented on record.

Gene joined Benny Goodman in 1934 and his influence affected all who followed, to include the type of equipment and drum sizes that he played on. He helped standardize the drum set up that many jazz drummers still use today: 24 or 26" bass drum, 14" snare drum, 9X13 small tom mounted on the shell of the bass drum, and 16" floor tom. In a 1938 metronome magazine, Gene talked about his cymbal set up.

At my left I have a 13" medium Zildjian. On the bass drum I have an eight-inch Chinese and a very heavy 14" Zildjian. I have the last one there because it doesn't ring too much when I play on it with the end of a stick. Over on my right I have a 16" medium.

From the same Metronome issue, he talks about his hi-hat cymbals:

I always thought my cymbals had been made in Turkey, but just a week or so ago Mr. Zildjian, himself, dropped in, and after examining them told me they were made right here. I still like them, though. They are 11-inch matched, a bit heavier then paper thin. I want to suggest to all of you who are going to buy high hats to be sure not to get them too high-pitched. They should have a fairly deep tonal quality, otherwise they'll sound tinny.

With the exception of some of the cymbal sizes and bass drum size, this set up is still in use by many big band drummers and is very economical in terms of physically moving around the instrument. In addition to developing this all purpose drum set up, he helped develop tom toms that were tunable with a drum key on both sides. He also was responsible for the white marine pearl drum finish that many jazz drummers embraced including Buddy Rich. Before Krupa, all drum sets were covered with a black or white finish.

With the popularity of the 1937 Benny Goodman hit *Sing, Sing, Sing* (RCA), Krupa was one of the first jazz musicians to play extended solos to high critical acclaim.

On the following page is a transcription from the introduction to "Sing, Sing, Sing" from the *Live at Carnegie Hall Concert of 1938*. To see the complete transcription, turn to page 176.

With Benny Goodman, this was the first time a drummer became a personality with a band as a sideman. At the time, if you wanted to be known as a drumming star, you had to be the leader of the band, like Chick Webb did.

A month after the famed Carnegie Hall concert, Krupa left Goodman to form his own orchestra that he led into the early 1940's. After his group disbanded, he returned to Goodman's orchestra in 1943 and then to Tommy Dorsey's band in late 1943.

In early 1944, he began making plans to form a new orchestra with a new sound. Being influenced by the music of Charlie Parker and Dizzy Gillespie, Krupa made a commitment to this new music and decided to form one of the first large ensembles to play it. During this period, Gene listened closely to young be-bop drummers like Kenny Clarke, Max Roach, and Roy Haynes and tried to alter his swing style to fit the music. For swing drummers, the time was played on the hi-hat and bass drum. For the new wave of drummers, the focal point became the ride cymbal. The conception that the be-bop drummers brought was a melodic one and the drum set was used to color the arrangement, filling holes and adding rhythmic comments. The time feel was also much lighter and the drum sizes tended to be smaller. A typical be-bop drum set consists of an 18" bass drum, 12" mounted tom, and a 14" large tom.

On the following page are (5) two measure comping examples extracted from the alto and trombone choruses from *Disc Jockey Jump*. They illustrate Gene's attempt to transition into the new be-bop style. It's interesting to note however, that during the trumpet choruses which occur after the drum solo breaks; he reverts back to his "comfort zone" by accompanying the trumpet solo on the hi-hat in a traditional manner.

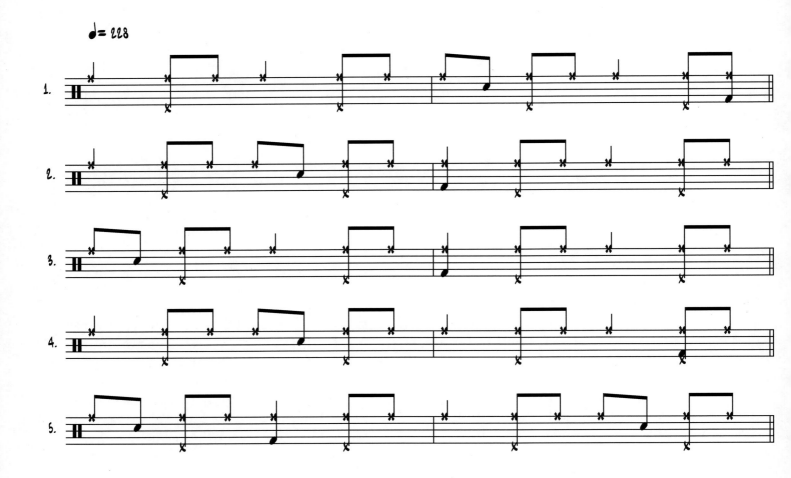

Krupa continued to lead his be-bop big band until 1951. The last 22 years of his life he mainly entertained as a solo personality with Norman Granz's Jazz at the Philharmonic, and appeared in three motion pictures that dealt with the big band era: The Glenn Miller Story, The Benny Goodman Story, and a film detailing his own life entitled The Gene Krupa Story.

I won the Gene Krupa drum contest in 1941. He watched me come up and develop. He was a dear man. He had a wonderful personality. Buddy and I both loved Gene. He was the guy who brought drums to the foreground. Before Gene, the drummer was always in the background. He made it a solo instrument and brought it forward. He made the importance of the drum and drummer stand out, what it means to have a great drummer in a band. You can have a mediocre band and a great drummer and that band will sound great, but if you have a great band and a mediocre drummer, the band will sound mediocre. That doesn't come off too well. The drum chair in a band is the hot seat. All those great drummers that I mentioned they took command, they listened, they had the ability to play according to the music. That's why they were so great. What I like about them too is they pass on their knowledge that they learned to other drummers. That's why young players today should know about these drummers.

Personal interview with Louie Bellson

*Jo Jones circa
1975*

When Jo Jones joined the Count Basie Orchestra in 1934, the role of drummer in the rhythm section changed. With Walter Page on bass, Freddie Green on rhythm guitar, and Count Basie on piano, the "All American Rhythm Section" was born. Their conception of playing time was an innovation all its own. This new approach was soft and light, yet intense. It was strong and also relaxed with each member contributing as a part of a rhythm team. Before the Basie rhythm section approach, the time was directed solely by the drummer and everyone in the ensemble followed. Consequently, the ensemble's feel at times could be heavy handed and ponderous. The magic of the Basie rhythm section was the blend they achieved. Through experimentation, they discovered that if they played at a certain dynamic level and internalized the subdivisions together as a unit, they could create a new texture.

Jo Jones, a contemporary of Gene Krupa and Dave Tough, was born in Chicago in 1911 and spent most of his time growing up in Alabama. His first experience with Basie came at the start of 1934 as a member of Benny Moten's Band. After Moten's death, many of his men joined Basie to include Jones, Lester Young, and Herschel Evans.

Basie's new rhythm section gave an identity to the band. Jo Jones defined Basie's swing feel by playing time on the hi-hat cymbals. He mastered this instrument and was aptly crowned "Mr. hi-hat" due to his ability to set tempos on them. If you view old video footage of Jo Jones with Basie from the 30's and 40's as well as Buddy Rich with Artie Shaw, you will notice that the hi-hat stand was non-adjustable. At that time, the standard hi-hat cymbal size was 10, 11, or 12". Jo Jones used larger cymbals which created a new sound. His 13" cymbals produced a deeper *chaw* sound on the strong beats of one and three and a wider *chick* accent on beats two and four. The innovation of using larger hi-hat cymbals producing a more defined and articulate beat changed the character of the drum set. Drummers slowly became time players on *cymbals* as they moved away from the Dixieland time playing approach on the snare drum.

Quotes

"Papa Jones laid the groundwork...I feel the same about all the guys I've known in my life time because each one was an individual stylist...Jo sounded like Jo, and Gene sounded like Gene, Philly Joe sounded like Philly, and Max sounded like Max."

"When a guy is standing up to play a solo, it's your function to make him play...Not to lay back, but not to overshadow him either. It's a fine line between being intrusive, and subtly hip. When I hear the applause he gets, I'm totally statisfied."

Buddy Rich, Modern Drummer
Dec/Jan 1980

On the first chorus of Basie's piano solo on *Honeysuckle Rose* from the *Complete Original American Decca Recordings,* he plays on the closed hi-hat and the hi-hat stand. Due to the composition of the stand, which in those days was made of nickel, the sound of the stand resembles a tiny bell ringing.

This example illustrates the beat Jo Jones played on the A sections of the first solo chorus.

On the bridge of the piano solo, he plays this idea on the stand and closed hi-hat.

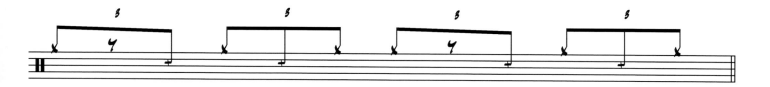

On the last A section, he plays the traditional hi-hat pattern closed with his right hand and beats two and four with his left hand on the stand.

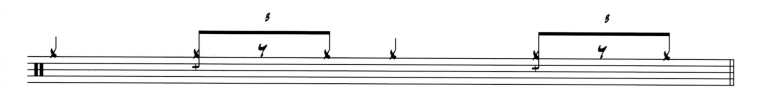

Below are examples he plays during the second piano chorus of *Honeysuckle Rose.*

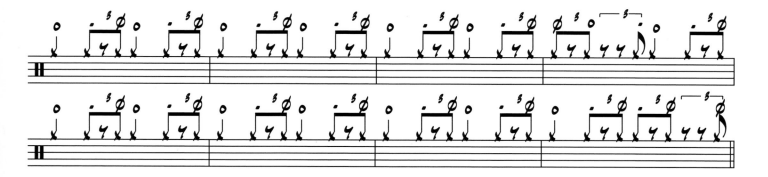

For an example of Jo Jones solo style, check out his (6) drum solo breaks from the track *Lopin'* from the *Original American RCA-Victor Recordings*. His approach is part rudimental, mixed with legato eighth note ideas.

Drum solo transcription example of Lopin'-Jo Jones

Mr. Basie wanted the drummer to SWING first and foremost. He liked it when the drums would kick the band hard in ensemble work and also set up the figures. You had to absolutely be aware of the dynamics and have a command of everything from pp (maybe even ppp) to FFF moving between all levels in a New York minute.

In the Basie band it was imperative that the drums and guitar were pretty much locked in with each other. That wasn't too difficult for me -- I just kept my ears and one eye on Freddie Green. There's not much call for that situation outside of Basie. Bands in the 30's and some 40's always had a rhythm guitar but that's pretty much fallen by the wayside now. As far as fitting in that section, Basie just told me one thing but it was enormously important. That one thing? He only said "LISTEN". You must listen to the section as a whole and the band as a whole and then react.

Basie taught me about one hundred million important things, in jazz and in life. Musically, for a drummer, sometimes it's more important to leave some breathing room and space for the band than it is to fill every single little vacuum in an arrangement. LEARN WHAT NOT TO PLAY! Papa Jo and Gus Johnson were masters at this.

Personal Interview with Butch Miles

Buddy Rich-Big Swing Face

Buddy Rich circa 1984

Buddy Rich was a product of Vaudeville. He began his professional career at 18 months performing Stars and Stripes Forever as the finale in his parents act. At age 3 he became a permanent part of their show. Buddy was an entertainer who could tap dance, sing, and act but more importantly, he led one of the greatest big bands in history from 1966-1986. His power, energy, and consistency each and every performance was extraordinary.

In 1938 he joined clarinetist Joe Marsala followed by a short stint with Bunny Berigan's Band. The following year, he joined Artie Shaw's Orchestra and later that year Tommy Dorsey. Buddy stayed with Dorsey for seven years and with vocalist Frank Sinatra, helped make the big band era a sensation.

In 1946, he led his first big band and the following year employed Stanley Kay as his assistant drummer at the Sherman Hotel in Chicago. In an interview I conducted with Mr. Kay, he spoke about the first time he met Buddy at the Hickory House in New York with Joe Marsala.

Buddy was playing with Joe Marsala at the Hickory House on 52nd Street in New York. It was a Sunday afternoon jam session that ran from 3-6pm. Joe Marsala played clarinet, his brother Marty played trumpet, his wife Adele Girard was the harpist, Nat Chappy played piano, and Artie Shapiro was on bass. I went over and introduced myself to Buddy before the jam session started. He knew my sister Cybil Kay, who was also a child star that worked with Buddy when they were both seven and eight years old. She went on to sing professionally with Benny Goodman and Woody Herman. She called Buddy to let him know that I would be over to see him and when I arrived, he said kid, go sit over there. After all the other drummers sat in, it was around 5:30 when Buddy played Jim Jam Stomp which was a flag waiver. I listened, and I'll tell you, I never heard drumming like that before in my entire life. From then on, I idolized him. Morning, noon, or night, if he was playing, I was there...

I read in a Downbeat magazine that Artie Shaw was looking for a drummer because Cliff Leman had left the band. Shaw played at the Lincoln Hotel and I waited in the alley way for him to come out. When he did, I went up to him and said Mr. Shaw, I read that you are looking for a drummer and I know the best in the world. He said, who's that and I told him Buddy Rich. He can't play kid was his reply. About a week later, Buddy was in the band and I felt that I got him the job.

Stanley also spoke about how he was hired by Buddy to be his assistant drummer:

In 1947, I got a call to join Buddy's band at the Sherman Hotel in Chicago. I get to Chicago, and go to his suite to meet with him around 4:00pm. He directed me to go over to the band hotel across the street, get changed, and play the first set for him at seven o'clock. So I get to the Sherman Hotel early, around 6pm, and I get on the band stand and the guys on the band said where are you going? I told them I was the new drummer in the band and there reply was WHAT? Are you here to steal his drums? Buddy never told the band that he was hiring an assistant drummer. So I joined the band incognito so to speak.

For an example of Buddy's style during this period, listen to the Tommy Dorsey recording *That Sentimental Gentleman*. Buddy's drums were recorded with remarkable audio quality. You can hear the influence of Gene Krupa and Chick Webb in the ideas and overall approach on this disc.

Throughout the 1950s, Buddy recorded with Art Tatum, Count Basie, and Charlie Parker. He also led small groups, toured with Jazz at the Philharmonic, and led a septet in 1960 that introduced vibraphonist Mike Mainieri.

In 1962, Rich joined the Harry James Orchestra in Las Vegas and stayed with James until forming his own band in early 1966. I spoke with trombonist and arranger Phil Wilson about this period of Buddy's career and his years with Harry James.

In 1963, the Woody Herman Band played for a month at the Castaways Casino in Las Vegas, and on our nights off which were once a week, or when we had some time to ourselves, Jake Hanna and I would go over to the Flamingo Hotel where the Harry James Band had a long running engagement and Buddy Rich was his drummer. Jake and I would sit in the back of the lounge when Harry's Band came on and it was just unbelievable. Those guys were playing so tight with Ray Simms on trombone, and Willie Smith on lead alto. It was a wonderful band, and on comes Buddy Rich, and he sits down behind his drums and plays like you and I wish we could. So relaxed. He was the highest paid sideman in the jazz business that year and he was happy with not a care in the world. You should have heard him play! Two words sum Buddy up, fire and inspiration. When he played like that, it was more of a certain happiness that he was conveying. Buddy was obviously happy in what he was doing and it came across in his playing. It wasn't aggressive like so many drummers, it was right down the middle and that particular era of his playing was extremely happy. Jake loved Buddy Rich. That was his number one drummer and he'd be the first to tell you as would many drummers and they'd be right.

In 1966, Buddy hired some of the finest young musicians in the country and enlisted such arrangers as Oliver Nelson, Bill Holman, Phil Wilson, and Bill Potts to compose original compositions and arrangements tailored to fit Buddy's physical style of drumming. He wanted to form a band that played modern music.

Buddy would try to burn out a young band. A bunch of Berklee kids that were in their early 20's. He would let you know in no uncertain terms that it was his band. His favorite quote was "I want the loudest band in the world." The band was use to that up on top of the beat feel and so when a drum sub came in, they didn't have that energy. First of all, they were dealing with having to learn the music right there. Anybody is at a disadvantage trying to deal with a brand new situation, but then on top of learning the music, you're substituting for this dynamo kind of an individual. NOBODY could play Buddy's music the way he did and could. He had arrangers that wrote the book around him. They wrote the ever popular West Side Story Medley and Channel One Suite... He had incredible chops, but his energy no matter how he was feeling, his energy was always right up on top. He had all those special accents that were right with the arrangement.

Personal interview with Walt Namuth, guitarist with Buddy Rich from 1968-1972

Buddy Rich's innovation to the music was his energy force and technique. His time from beat to beat was impeccable and if you listen closely to the phrasing of his ensemble, they play with a very crisp approach, very much akin to the way Buddy played his snare drum.

To hear Buddy at his best, check out the recordings he did on the Pacific Jazz label. Some of my favorites are Swingin' New Big Band, Live at the Chez; Big Swing Face; Mercy Mercy; The New One; and Keep the Customer Satisfied.

Stanley Kay

Buddy Rich
"In Clinic," 1970

Mel Lewis circa 1960

Mel Lewis was born in Buffalo, NY and began playing professionally at age fifteen. His first drumming influence was his father who worked as a pit drummer for shows that came through Buffalo. Other influences include Dave Tough, Tiny Kahn, and Gus Johnson. Mel first came to prominence when he joined Stan Kenton's Orchestra in 1954. His drumming style was different than his contemporaries. He used smaller drums that resembled what a be-bop drummer of the period would play. He also favored dark cymbal sounds that blended with the ensemble as opposed to bright, cutting sounds. He was known for not using crash cymbals and believed that each cymbal should have crash qualities and an accompaniment purpose. Like Dave Tough, he loved the roaring sound of the Chinese cymbal and equally detested flashy drum solos.

In a 1985 interview in Modern Drummer magazine, Mel spoke in depth about his cymbal concept and sound.

I find that all the cymbals should be dark. High-pitched cymbals have a tendency to obliterate high sounds. So when you hit a high crash cymbal with the brass section while they're up in that high register, you will knock out half their sound. Trombones, of course, can go lower than my cymbals can, so I want to be somewhere in the middle register where I don't obliterate the lead and I don't destroy the bottom. With the saxophones, you want a roaring sound to envelope, because reeds don't have the power that the brass has. That's why I believe that during a sax soli, nothing sounds better behind them than a Chinese ride cymbal...

When you've got a whole ensemble, you want a strong, enveloping, low sound with a lot of clari-

ty as far as the beat is concerned. It's like a picture with a beautiful metal frame around it. It gives tremendous fullness to the sound of the band.....

Every cymbal you have should be a ride cymbal, because you should treat the different sections with a different ride behind it. There is nothing worse than the monotony of one cymbal going on behind everything. When the band is playing along and they keep hearing the same cymbal sound, it just disappears in their minds. But when you make a change to another ride cymbal, it wakes them up again. Even in my dark sounds there is still a higher sound, a medium sound, and a lower sound.

Mel was nicknamed the tailor because he had a knack for making all the parts of a big band arrangement fit together perfectly. For this reason, he was respected and sought after by every conceivable big band arranger of the time to include Bill Holman and Marty Paich. His beat was also different. He played with a loose triplet feel like Dave Tough, but his ideas were linear, meaning he didn't layer repetitive rhythms or ostinatos with his four limbs like most drummers. You can hear this approach which has come to be known as the "rub a dub dub" feel on countless recordings that he is on.

In a conversation with Danny Gottlieb, he spoke about his experiences studying with Mel, and his approach.

My personal contact with him actually started through Joe Morello. I heard Mel one night at the Vanguard, and as I was studying with Joe, thought it might be a good idea to take a few lessons with Mel as well. When I asked him, he was very nice, but said he was just too busy to teach. I left the Vanguard a little depressed, and at a lesson with Joe soon after, I told him of my experience.

Joe said, "I know Mel. Call him up, and I'll talk to him for you!" I promptly got Mel's number from the NY Musician's Union, and called him from Dorn and Kirshner's, the store where Joe was teaching.

Joe got on the phone with Mel, and said "I have this student, who loves your ride cymbal, would you get together with him?" And Mel gave in, and said it was ok to come to his house. I think I had just gotten my driver's license, so I was 17 and that would make this 1970. Mel lived in Irvington, New York, and Joe lived in Irvington, New Jersey, so it was kind of a bizarre connection.

That one phone call started a series of many days spent together, talking drums, music and life. It was just unbelievable! Mel would play recordings (many that are now available on cd) from his private collection, and I remember lugging a Teac Reel to Reel tape recorder to his house to make copies.

As far as the "rub-a dub" approach, I remember Mel talking about it, and he refers to it in the interviews with Loren Schoenberg, but for me it was working with Bobby Brookmeyer that kind of solidified the concept. After Mel passed away, Bobby would hire me for a variety of projects with the WDR Big Band in Cologne, Germany- projects that Mel would have done. I remember once Bobby saying that I should fill using Mel's concept, the "Rub-a Dub", where

1) You played where the band doesn't play, and

2) You filled using mainly the 8th note pulse, already being generated by the rhythm section.

I remember at the time, I was playing some of the figures in unison with the band (maybe Buddy Rich style), and Bobby felt that (in my case) it was making the figures sound stiff. If I were to fill in the holes, especially with 8th notes, it would help solidify the rhythm section and the figures. And, you know, it always seems to work!

222

I didn't appreciate it fully when I heard Mel, and spent time with him, but if you listen to his recordings today, it is almost IMPOSSIBLE to find an example where Mel is ahead or behind the band. There is virtually NO fill or figure that is off from the band. NONE! I don't think I can find ONE recording of myself that doesn't have something a little ahead, or behind. But not Mel. It's unbelievable. And the question is, WHY? In my opinion, it's because his feel is so embedded in the time, and all the fills use the Rub-a Dub approach. Since you are following the 8th note pulses, and not straying too much, you are always in the center of the time. That way, you are really connected to all instruments in the band, in a very deep way.

On the following page is an early example of Mel's rub a dub dub beat with the Stan Kenton Orchestra from 1954. As you examine the ensemble figures in the upper staff, notice how Mel's rhythmic activity takes place when the band is resting.

With Danny Gottlieb

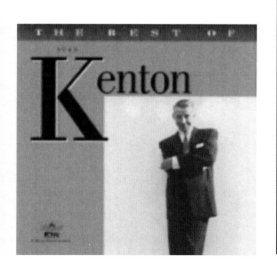

Stompin' at the Savoy ensemble figure interpretation transcription-Mel Lewis

Mel re-located to Los Angeles in 1957 and co-led a combo with arranger Bill Holman. He also worked and recorded with the Terry Gibbs Big Band. Hearing Mel on these "dream band" recordings are some of his finest work.

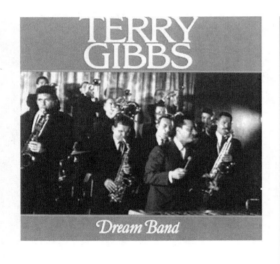

He returned to New York for good in 1963 and in late 65, he and trumpeter Thad Jones formed the Thad Jones-Mel Lewis Orchestra. Jones left the band to move to Denmark in 1978 and Mel continued to lead the group until his passing on February 2nd 1990. The band continues the tradition every Monday night at the Village Vanguard in New York City.

This collection of interviews has taken place over the course of several years. I spoke with drummers as well as composers, arrangers, and other instrumentalists asking for their insights and experiences working for legendary big band leaders. My objective is for young musicians to read this and learn from these historical accounts, appreciating the sacrifices that were made for the love of music.

Louie Bellson

I had already written *Skin Deep* when I joined Duke Ellington. I wrote it while I was on Tommy Dorsey's Band. Tommy didn't play any of my charts because he respected me as a drummer. I had finished Skin Deep by the time I joined Duke's Band and he said "Hey, I heard you write arrangements? Bring them in!" At first I said, wow, me bring in an arrangement to this organization? I was reluctant at first. But Duke kept saying bring it in. Finally, Juan Tizol said "Duke wants you to bring your music in." So I reluctantly brought in The Hawk Talks first and then Skin Deep and Duke recorded both of them. It was really something. Skin Deep was recorded in a ballroom. Duke sent the tape to the recording studio in New York and the engineers said we can't do any better then this, referring to the quality of the sound. Duke was afraid to go into the studio with that arrangement at that time because he didn't know if the engineers would be able to get the clarity of the snare drum on tape because of all the beats I was playing.

It was an honor for me to play in that band. It was an unusual band. Collectively we played so well together and yet each member were individual stylists. I never heard that kind of sound before. It was very different for me. Duke inspired me to do a lot of things, that's why I'm still writing and playing today. The other bands I worked with were great too: Tommy Dorsey, Benny Goodman, and Count Basie. They were all great. But Duke had extra lions that the others didn't have. This enabled him to get further into the music.

Time Feel

I listen to the music I'm playing, and I don't change the equipment I use. For example, change out my bass drum or use a different snare drum. I use the same equipment whether I'm playing with a trio, duet, or a big band. The important thing for me is to learn what the music is all about. I may be playing an arrangement that will require me to use one bass drum, and then turn around for a different arrangement that requires the two bass drums and I do that. Listen to what the music is all about and play accordingly. That's very important. When I worked with Oscar Peterson's trio, he would say "more wood Lou." I would start off with brushes on a tune and by the time we got to the shout chorus he would say give me the wood, more wood. A certain loudness can be musical. When it gets to the point where its noise, then you're not doing it. When it's loud, intense, and musical, then you've got it.

On Buddy Rich

The snare drum is a very important instrument. Buddy and I both worked hard on playing the snare drum for years. Buddy and I were great friends and we played drum battles together and it was competitive, but a love competitive. He understood what I was doing and I understood what he was doing. We both challenged one another and brought the drums up to a level where we thought it should be. That is the way I play today. I give over 100% and Buddy did the same thing. We always had fun doing it. That's the joy of playing drums or any other instrument is to have fun doing it. It was never mean spirited between Buddy and me. We got along great and had a mutual respect for one another. He wrote something in a book once about me. The interviewer asked him "what do you think of Louie Bellson?", he said well, first of all, everyone knows that Louie is a great player, but the thing that knocks me out is that we've been friends for 35 years and that means a lot. His complement on our friendship really stayed with me because when you're friends, that covers a lot of territory. It makes your playing stand out. When you play with Buddy, you better have your boots raised because he'll let you have it. Man, I miss him...

On Technique

It came naturally to me to play hard with intensity, but yet relaxed. That sounds kind of funny to say, you play with intensity yet relaxed. I learned to do that when I went to Japan the first time. They were amazed. When you push the drum set, you push it with love. Every note you play should mean something. When you play with that much force, and yet relaxed, that's the way to do it. You can get a guy that weighs 300 lbs, a muscle man, and put sticks in his hands and ask him to hit the snare drum and he'll hit it hard. I can walk up to the same drum and just BAM and my sound will be much more forward than his. You have to know how to hit a drum. I learned that at a very early age.

On Jo Jones

The man who gave me more advice than anybody was Jo Jones. He was the kind of guy who could play with lots of intensity, and yet it was so relaxed. He was like a fan dancer the way he moved his arms. You felt comfortable with him. It's like going to an ice show and watching ice skaters perform, smooth and graceful, yet so powerful. He also taught me how to listen and play the brushes. Buddy and I both agreed that Jo Jones was the champ with brushes. He got a sound that no one could get. He also played the hi-hat beautifully.

When a soloist like Dizzy Gillespie is out front playing a solo, the drummer is the accompaniment, not the soloist. Dizzy is the soloist, but you have to make him sound good, and the way to make him sound good is to listen to every note he's playing. If he takes a breath for a bar and a half, that means a fill for you. It's so important to know how to play behind a soloist, and when it's time for you to solo, then you solo! The great ones know how to do this.

Max Roach taught me something... I did one of the first clinics with Max over 50 years ago. When he heard me play, he said Louie, you play so fantastic, do you ever think of the melody? After that, I started to listen to standards like Cottontail and I learned to play according to the melody. I learned that from Max. Keep the melody in mind. That way when you stretch out and solo, you're telling a story. It's very boring to hear a guy play a long drum solo and all he does is repeat technical ideas. When you hear a drummer play in phrases, and he knows where he is, defining one, when the solo is complete, you know you've heard something. When soloing, you don't have to play fortissimo all the time. You can play soft. Dynamics are extremely important. That's more effective than playing loud sometimes.

The process of learning a new arrangement

When I joined Duke Ellington's band, he didn't have a drum book at all. I had to join the band and listen intently to what they were doing. I had one advantage, I would sit by a trombone player like Juan Tizol and I could look at his music and tell where they were in the arrangement. By listening and not relying on reading with Duke, I learned the music faster because sometimes you can concentrate on reading a chart too much and it takes you away from listening to the band. A drummer in a big band needs to be a quick study. You should learn how to improvise and memorize fast because like I said before, all your concentration other wise is on reading the chart, you forget what is going on with the band.

Advice for young drummers

In closing, I would like to offer this to all the young drummers. Learn to play your instrument and make that a part of your life. Be open to listening to all kinds of recordings. Listen to all kinds of drummers to include the old timers and the young guys coming up because you can always walk into a club and sit down and listen to the drummer and learn something from him. Music is a learning process and everyday you wake up, you can open up a book and study the scales of drumming and do it with love because that's what I did. You learn to play and have fun. That's the important thing. There isn't a day that doesn't go by that I go out and hear a drummer play and say I like what he did there, I'm going to try that. Learn how to play different arrangements, learn how to improvise, and memorize fast. Those are all key things every drummer should know. It takes time and effort. Keep on schooling.

I'm very fortunate to still be able to go out and play a little bit. I'm not playing as much as I did when I was twenty years old but I get out and do a few dates each month. I put the sticks in my hand every day just to feel the instrument. That way when I go out and play, the instrument is not foreign to me, it's part of me. It's a joy to play.

I always mention the fact that you have to know where you came from in order to know where you're going. I don't know who coined that phrase but it sure is a good one. You have to know about Chick Webb, Davy Tough, Buddy Rich, Gene Krupa of course, and Shelly Manne. They were all great. You have to know these players and how they contributed to the music. To bring it up date, Steve Gadd, Dave Weckl, Dennis Chambers, and Vinnie Colauita. Every drummer should know these players. That's why I wrote that book *Their Time Was the Greatest*, 12 drummers, 6 old timers and 6 new guys. It's about doing your homework, really. These players had it all. If you don't know these players, you need to go back to the drawing board.

With Louie Bellson, 2004

If I recall right, I think Al Porcino was on trumpet on the *Mercy Mercy* record, and that helped out a great deal. Art Pepper was also on it. We did our band set at Ceasars at 8PM, followed by Tony Bennett's set, then a little bit of a break, followed by the recording. We got started well after midnight, probably around one or two in the morning. When we were done, the sun was up. That date was a typical Vegas adventure.

I would always sit just to the right of Buddy from the perspective of the drummer. I played a gig in London with the band. It was my first European tour in one of those ancient, very large concert halls where a symphony would play. It was called the Odeon Hammersmith. He was sitting on a riser that went up about 4' high, and then his drums towered above that, with his cymbal up here. His cymbals were right above my head, and the bass drum, which I think was a 26" drum, was at ear level with me. That bad boy was right at my head! The first rehearsal for that gig, I had to go out and buy some ear plugs because it was beyond description it was so loud. And this was one of those concert halls that was very live and loud. It was like echo all through the place.

On band sets

The sets varied according to what kind of mood he was in at the time and what he would pull up reflected that. A lot of times this was done on the stand and guys would be scrambling for a chart out of 150 or 200 pieces of music stacked 3' high. Sometimes he would give us a running start.....101! 98! 55!

Occasionally the parts would be falling apart because they've been played so many times. Anything could happen. When I went back with the band for the last time in 72, I spent a couple of hours looking for the guitar book.....there was none! What I found was several tattered parts. The book was torn apart with lost pages and lost parts. Maybe 20 to 30 charts gone!

Sherrie Maricle, drummer and leader of DIVA on studying with Mel Lewis

I studied with Mel Lewis for 1 year. He was, and is one of the most swingin', beautiful, powerful, sensitive, intuitive players I have ever had the joy of listening to. My lessons with him were far from conventional. Most of our time was spent in his New York City, West End Ave apartment listening to, discussing, evaluating and dissecting recordings...of Mel, all the great players you can name, and my very humble offerings. We also never failed to delve into the ups, downs, frustrations and joys of the music business. We never actually played together and I never saw a stick, drum pad or drum in his house, but the manner in which he shared his musical knowledge and experience transcended the need for learning via the traditional "tools of the trade". The most generous thing he ever did for me was to let me play the 3rd set at the Village Vanguard with The Mel Lewis Jazz Orchestra. Through all of its incarnations his band was, and is one of my favorites. I was wildly enthused over this unbelievable opportunity and will never forget that "first time" feeling of being part of a band that played so well together with such explosive power and finesse. I remember thinking...it feels like these guys are playing with 1 singular brain, or being driven by a singular force...so after the initial "oh-my-god" feeling, getting use to Mel's calf head and open loose bass drum, I started to settle in and revel in the groove. The best part of this experience was Mel being in the audience "teaching" me between tunes...mostly telling me to "play louder" and "relax". I'm glad nobody in the audience asked for their money back.

Mel provided me with many sage music, business, and life lessons that have helped me navigate these past 20 years as a musician in NYC. However, on those occasions when I was struggling with confidence, experiencing slumps in my playing or mad because I didn't "play the right thing" Mel would say, *"Only you know what you wanted to do, nobody else. Don't pay attention to what you wanted to do, enjoy what you did. It sounds great to me and in 100 years not even you will care."* I have quoted Mel many times over the years and have learned that in every moment of self-expression and creativity there is something good.

I played with the Glenn Miller Band under the direction of Ray McKinley for 3.5 years, 1960-1963. When I left the band, they were booked into Lake Tahoe for two and a half months. Ray kept calling and asked if I can do this because it was the first time the band was to the west coast and it would be a bad time to break in a new drummer. I kept telling him no because I've gotten it (being on the road) out of my system. Every time he called and asked, he kept raising the money. I'll pay you this and fly you out and at the end of the engagement, fly you back to North Carolina, so I agreed.

When we there working, the Harry James Band was right across the street at Harrah's and Buddy Rich was playing drums. So I got to hear Buddy Rich play every night of the week, 6 nights a week, for two and a half months. We got to be really good friends.

When I worked for Ray at the beginning, I was considered the "ballad drummer". I also played the tunes that backed Ray on vocals. He would do In the Mood, American Patrol, and all the big numbers. By the time I got off the band, I was playing everything.

We carried one drum set. I'm 5'8" and Mac was 6'4'. We used one of those old pearl covered drum thrones that all the companies made in those days. McKinkley had Ludwig make his 6" taller to accommodate his height which made the throne 30" tall! For me, it was like practically standing up to play. Before I joined the band, I'd been playing a little be-bop Gretsch set with the cymbals titled. I picked up one of those drum thrones from Ludwig and had it cut down so I was only sitting 20" high. The drums we used were Ludwig: 22" Bass Drum, 9x13 and 16x16 toms, and a 5x14 metal snare drum. The cymbals were Zildjian. A 20" ride, two 16" crash cymbals, and a pair of 14" hi-hats. The top hi-hat cymbal was thin and the bottom medium.

On hi-hat playing

From time to time, I go back and listen to the things Ray did on those records. He was one of the best hi-hat cymbal players that I ever heard in my life. I didn't realize at the time what I was hearing or listening to. Some nights, Ray McKinley could absolutely BURN the drum set to pieces. On the nights he was really up to play, it was just absolutely gorgeous.

When he kept time, he would stomp the hell out of the bass drum. He came from that era, back in the 30's and 40's when all drummers played like that. We didn't use a wooden bass drum beater, we used a felt beater on a Speed King pedal. We had 6 or 8 of those pedals on the bus.

On working for a leader

Ray didn't want the cymbal sound to hang over past a band figure. He didn't like any fills played into a figure or behind a vocalist either. I go back and listen to some of the records I did and think, boy that would have been nicer if I had been permitted to play a fill there.

He didn't like it when I would play set ups or fills into a band figure. He rarely did it himself. Ray liked straight time.

Great recordings to listen to of Ray's playing are with Jimmy Dorsey, Will Bradley, and also the Glenn Miller Army Air Force Band. I always prided myself on being a drummer that never studied, but when I look back, I studied under one of the masters for 3.5 years!

When I first joined the band, we used calf skin heads believe it or not. Ray was old fashioned. When I met Joe Calato for the first time he gave me some nylon tip sticks to try but Ray would have nothing to do with them. He liked the sound of a wood tip stick better. When we started to do the Glenn Miller Time TV specials at the Ed Sullivan Theater in NYC for CBS, we switched from calf skin to plastic drum heads after a while and Ray learned to like them.

For the most part, he was a super guy and the band respected him. However, one night I almost got fired! I was playing one of the things, I don't know, not In the Mood, but an arrangement like that. I was really pushing it, (the time that is) and the manager Lenny Hambro got up out of the saxophone section and he and Ray came back and just read me the riot act about rushing. My principal on the thing was I figured the guy that wrote and arranged the chart had a tempo in mind and that's why he wrote those figures that way. Ray's response was, "well, let's not forget who the bandleader is!" And that was the end of that conversation...

Ray was never a ride cymbal player as such. He could really WORK the hi-hats. It was like listening to Jo Jones with the Basie Band. He wasn't a great technician as such. The drums were tuned kind of loose because of the articulation. A loose snare drum can cover up a lot of mistakes. We were in Columbus, Ohio one night for their home coming dance. The headline entertainment was Peter Nero with Joe Cusatis on drums. I was talking with Joe and he asked if it would be cool if he used my drums rather than bring all his stuff in, and I said sure. Well, he came off the band stand after his set with Nero and said how in the hell do you play that equipment! Joe kept his drums tight and he used a small set of Slingerlands, I think. And here we had a 16" and 13" tom toms tuned really loosely and the bass drum was a big booming sound.

Ray always wanted me to play four on the floor ALL the time. When I left the band and came back to North Carolina, it took me several years to get that approach out of my system.

If Ray didn't play the way he played, you wouldn't be playin' the way you play, because it all had to start somewhere and it didn't start with Neil Peart...

Ray McKinley
Freedomland Ballroom, New York City, 1961

231

Woody Herman, like Buddy Rich (They both came up through vaudeville.) could be rightfully caustic when the situation called for it.

The band had a really good paying gig at a country club in St. Louis; a Debutante party, or something like that. The band had been playing gigs at Elks Lodges for a pittance and this was important for Woody felt it could lead to more $$$$ gigs.

Our bus driver had a fine taste for controlled substances and he frequently lost his way on the way to gigs. True to form, we got to this one about 30 minutes before the starting time. The set up crew worked feverishly and the band was ready to begin at the appointed time. Everyone, that is, but the drummer who was leisurely selecting his sticks. Woody shot the ray and said loudly, "Soph, make sure you find some tonight that have some time in them." Woody had a way of bringing one back to earth and reality. He was a great man who cared deeply for the men who played his music. He ran one of the toughest universities in the business!

Trombonist Phil Wilson on drummer Jake Hanna and Woody Herman

Jake Hanna is a GREAT drummer, much larger than so many people realize in his steadiness. You can play tempos with him and you would feel comfortable. That's how tempos like Caldonia came off. That was incredible, and as a trombone player I will take exception... I think I know it a little more than you do. We all tried to play our eighth notes like Sal Nistico did. When he first came on the band he was 18 or 19, he was a bull! To listen to him play, all of us loved his playing and I'm not kidding when I say that we were all trying to play our eighth notes like him. Sal had a great time feel, and when you listen to any of the recordings, you'll hear the tight time of the ensemble. That was inspired by Sal. Bill Chase, who played lead trumpet, also influenced the way the band felt as did the rhythm section which was burnin'!

Playing with Woody was an incredible lesson for me. In roughly 1958 or 59, Woody had to dissolve his big band because he wasn't getting enough work. He scaled down the band to a small group with Bill Chase on trumpet, Woody played alto, Gordon Brisca on tenor, Nat Pierce on piano, Chuck Andreas on bass (Charlie the arm), and Jake on drums. This group played smaller clubs in the very early 60's. I ran into them when they were playing the Red Rooster Club in Detroit. I was in the Army playing in the NORAD Band and both groups just so happened to be playing Detroit at the same time. That was an interesting meeting because Bill Chase, Paul Fontaine from the NORAD Band, and I knew one other from back in 1955 when we were all attending the Berklee School of Music in Boston. By March of 1962, I got out of the Army and by that time, Nat Pierce had talked Woody Herman into starting a big band again and Nat offered to manage it. So Bill Chase assembled and called his old friends from Berklee College of Music. All in all, there were 12 of us who came out of Herb Pomeroy's (B) Band at Berklee that ended up joining Woody in 1962. It was like a family reunion because we hadn't seen each other in 7+ years! That was quite a gathering of guys who really loved each other. The band started playing gigs in May of 62 and in October of that year, we recorded *Woody Herman 1963, Swingest Big Band Ever*. A classic record, and now you know why....

There were two leaders in the history of big bands that were loved by the musicians that played under them. They were Woody and Count Basie. There was genuine love.

Gary Hobbs on working with Stan Kenton

Playing drums on Stan Kenton's band in the mid 70's was one of the best jobs a young drummer could wish for. The band was on the road 48 weeks a year and most of the gigs were one-nighters. The mode of travel was Stan's privately owned bus with "No Where" shown in the destination window above the wind shield. The gigs were a mixture of school concert/clinics, jazz clubs, and a few dances. The band was 19 pieces strong.

Those playing on this band developed the ability to perform at a very high level no matter how they felt. They may have felt sick or they may have been sick and tired of playing the same charts many nights in a row. They may have been sick and tired of playing and traveling with certain individuals on the band. We were always in some state of tiredness...

The drummer, unlike the 3rd trumpet or 4th trombone players, was encouraged to try new things nightly and that freedom made the drum chair a great place to develop new ideas and work on all of the things needed to become a better musician. The jazz players on the band were depending on you to help them create their solos. The ensemble needed you to drive them and to make sure that the dynamic contrasts were observed. The time and feel were in your hands. At times, those "times" were odd such as 7/8, 9/4, and 11/8. There was also room for drum solos nightly.

After 2 1/2 years of traveling on the road with the Stan Kenton Orchestra, I was transformed from a good young drummer into a seasoned professional with the awareness of all the things I have mentioned above. Stan was the man who insisted that the drummer on his band take control, offering up fresh material that would take the music to new heights nightly. I consider myself to have been very fortunate to have been in the right place at the right time and to have experienced this great environment for growth and learning.

Arranger and trombonist Bob Curnow on Stan Kenton

These were the drummers I worked with in the Kenton Band:

As a player: Dee Barton, 1963

As a Producer, Composer or Arranger:
Jerry Lestock McKenzie (1972)
Peter Erskine (1972-74)
Gary Hobbs (1975-77)

I'm probably forgetting someone for sure. Obviously, all of these players were very different, one from the other.

Dee's time was great most of the time ..... not a very technical player .... always exciting to watch and hear .... perfect for the band at that time, I thought. Fun to play with.

Jerry was back on the band for a short time while I was writing and rehearsing the "National Anthems" double LP in 1971-72. He was always a great friend to me. Most of his time with the band was before I played on it. He never had the chance to record the anthems because he left and Pete (Erskine) came on.

Pete then did about 4 albums with Stan and me. He was as thrilling then as he is now...... long, black hair flying around ...... the consummate '70's drummer, never any problem with Pete in any way. I love the guy. Always brings everything he has to the music.

Gary was also perfect for the band in the mid-late 70's. He was so incredibly exciting to hear then and also now (maybe even more so today). His time was/is impeccable. He played in my short-lived Seattle Big Band for about 2 years (2000-02), and I was always anxious to hear him play at the next rehearsal.

As far as my experience with Stan and how it shaped me .... frankly, it was just about everything to me. I started listening to that band when I was 13 years old and never stopped. He and I met when I was in college and I joined the band the day I graduated from college. I spent a year with the band in the trombone section and then went back to work with him about 8-9 years later as a writer, producer, and manager of Creative World Records.

So, obviously, I did a lot of different things with and for Stan, and he was always encouraging, supportive and gracious. He may have shaped me as much as a band leader as he did a player or composer. It goes without saying that my business experience with him allowed me to create and sustain Sierra Music Publications for the past 30 years. So, I owe him damned near everything.

My time with the Kenton Orchestra has a long history.

My father, Randy Taylor was a fan right from the beginning in the early forties. While he was serving in England in 1944, his father/my grandfather recorded a radio broadcast and took it to a record store in Dayton Ohio and gave it to Stan on the condition that Stan write my dad in England. My dad was really surprised and overwhelmed by getting a letter from his hero. They became life-long correspondents and eventually became great friends. Stan's dedication to his fans and his music has always been an inspiration to me.

I first heard the band at home of course through recordings but the first time going to a concert in 1961 with the Mellophonium band made a huge impression. What a huge sound and a great swinging band that was!

I eventually went to North Texas to study jazz with the goal of trying to get on the band. While teaching at a Stan Kenton clinic in Toronto, I realized that the band didn't have a samba {which was quite popular at the time} so I wrote "Samba de Haps" that week. After the first run-through Stan asked, "Can I buy that?" and I said, "Hell, you can have it!" I was thrilled to hear my music played by the band that I grew up listening to!

Stan was very encouraging and ended up recording 3 of my charts on his last 2

albums. I was able to attend the recording sessions and conduct my arrangements which was another great experience. He also published my charts which gave me my start in the music publishing business.

I would have to say that Stan was a very strong leader but was always approachable by the musicians. Consequently the musicians would follow him anywhere and hold out that last chord forever!

My short time with the band was the highlight of my career and a huge influence on my life as a composer/arranger.

Differences and similarities between small and large ensemble playing:

In all cases, but especially in a sight reading situation, the drummer's objective is to help the band sound polished. The larger the group, the more possible weak players so, as the ensemble grows, the fills and set-ups simplify.

On Woody Herman

Playing night after night on the road with the Woody Herman band was a fantastic experience. Woody, by his own example, taught me that no matter how tough the travel or gig circumstances were, it was essential that I bring 100% commitment to the bandstand every night.

On the influence of Mel Lewis

The lessons I learned from Mel include:

When an ensemble plays full tilt the sound can get harsh, if the drummer keeps the dynamics a little lighter, the ensemble will sound warmer.

Playing all the figures forces the horns to phrase like the drummer and can make things stiff.

Playing in a way that connects the phrases is more swinging than simply making all the hits.

Keeping the right hand on the ride cymbal as much as possible helps the over-all flow.

A darker ride cymbal is easier for the band to lock up with, a ping cymbal is too staccato and makes the beat feel small.

Think like an orchestra conductor - try to maximize the drama in the music.

Buddy Rich, Woody Herman, Benny Goodman, Count Basie, Stan Kenton and Mel Tormé.

237

The 1962 band that Woody Herman had was one of the best of all time. It really was. Woody said it was his best band. I personally felt that the 1946 band was his best and so did Al Cohn.

We played some fast tempos. Bassist Chuck Andreas and Bill Chase on lead trumpet could really play those tempos. Without a bass player like Chuck, you couldn't do it. He played 4/4 time without an amplifier. He was something else. We were flying man.

On the Woody Herman *Live Encore* record, the tempo on Caldonia was half note ='s 196 beats per minute and we never played it that slow again. As the band grew, we played that arrangement even faster later on. It ended up being in one. The way we developed our endurance to play those fast tempos was we built it up gradually. Bill Chase would ask, "How fast can you play it?" I told him I can play it this fast over four bars, and this fast for a chorus, and this fast for the rest of the night. At first we opted for the third way, gradually building it up until we could play it at the tempo that at first we could only play over four measures. Eventually, we would be able to play that fast all night. Our lead tenor player Sal Nistico was always right on it. Once he left, we really couldn't play like that anymore. He was a monster. NOBODY ever played like Sal, ever! Not that I ever heard anyway. He ate up fast tempos and laid down the time doing it! He was the whole thing.

I started working for Woody in 1957. Bill Chase and pianist Nat Pierce were the ones who really put Woody's great band together. Bill got guys he liked, and Nat got his guys. Nat wanted Count Basie style guys, and Bill Chase wanted Maynard Ferguson style guys, so we combined them and what you hear on those great records is what we ended up with. We never really talked about concepts on how we were going to play an arrangement. We just went for it every night. Bill rehearsed the trumpet section, Nat brought in new arrangements, and Woody would count off the tempo and the rhythm section would go by itself.

Woody was the easiest guy in the world to work for. He was one of us. He liked hanging out with us at the bar. Most band leaders won't do that, they separate themselves but Woody was very, very friendly.

I used Slingerland Drums when I was on Woody's band. I had an 18" ride that I also used to crash on to my right and a Chinese cymbal to my left that I also rode on. I couldn't crash on that one because it was too thin, it would break if you did. I played a calf skin head on my snare drum on those records, and I still use calf on my snare drum today. The rest of the drums had plastic heads on them. It's just easier to tune plastic. If you tune a plastic head, you can get a softer, calf like sound and feel from them. Gene Krupa first showed me how to tune plastic heads. Even though Gene used plastic after they came out, he always got a calf like sound from them. George Wettling also knew how to tune a drum with plastic heads. George could get a great sound out of anything, even a table top. That guy had the best sound I ever heard. He was a GREAT drummer. Nick Fatool also had a great sound.

Growing up as a kid, I would go to the RKO Theatre and listen to all the bands that came through. I heard Buddy Rich, Shadow Wilson, Gene Krupa, you name them and I heard them. Gene was my favorite. Everybody liked Gene. Davy Tough loved Gene Krupa, Buddy did too, and so did Jo Jones. I knew Gene very well. We used to go to mass every Sunday morning together. Gene was a great guy.

I stayed with Woody for almost a year in 1957, and then I left and went with Maynard Ferguson in 1958. I eventually got back with Woody in early 1962 and stayed with him until he ran out of music and patience.

When we played ensemble phrases, I always "keyed in" on how Bill Chase was swinging and phrasing a line. I listened to him all the time. He set the tone and phrasing. We were always exactly together. We grew up together in Boston. Bill was a real task master with the trumpet section in Woody's Band. He rehearsed them all the time. The guys in the section would often get tired of it. He was nice about it, never mean. It shows on the records. It was a very exciting band to play with and listen to. When we hit, it would scare the living hell out of you. Nobody could believe it, Benny Goodman included. The best records are the live ones that we did: *Encore, Woody Live at Basin Street West, and Woody's Goodies*. I felt that Woody's Goodies was the best one because it has throw away tunes from the other sessions. They were done out here on the west coast at Wilt Chamberlain's club Basin Street West.

We got a great time feel throughout the band due to the key players that I've mentioned: Bill Chase on lead trumpet, Sal Nistico on tenor, and Chuck Andreas on bass. We use to call Andreas "Charlie the Arm" because he was always right on the time. No matter who pushed, we were always together and in sync. These guys all had impeccable time.

I would have to say that my experiences playing with Woody's band was some of the best music I ever made with the best big band I ever played with. The thing we had with that band was monstrous. We worked the Metro Pole club in New York and because of the size of the room, we needed to set up "single file". So one night on the road, we were working in Lake Tahoe, Nevada and they had us set up like Harry James Band with the drums set up on a riser way up high and in the back of the band. We couldn't

make any kind of a sound together. We sounded pathetic because we got use to the single file way that we always used. So Woody had us tear down the bandstand and he put the saxes next to the drums, the trombones were next to my hi-hat, and the trumpet section went behind the drums, and the piano in front of the saxophone section. We were able to hear one another much better and we blew the walls down, it was fantastic! We called that set up the swingin' wedge or the swingin' V.

When we worked the Metro Pole, Shelly Manne came in to hear the band. He was working at the Vanguard with his group. He was so knocked out with the band that he got on the phone and called guys he knew, club owners across the country and within three hours, we were booked from New York to California. Jack Tracey came in the next day to record the band and we were off and running. That gig at the Metro Pole really got things started for us. That record was *Woody 63*. Our second recording was *Encore, Live at Basin Street West*. When we played Basin Street West, people were lined up around the block to come and hear us. Names like Henry Mancini, Johnny Mercer, Stan Kenton, you name it. The biggest names in music were waiting outside to hear this band. I couldn't believe it. We really didn't play anything new. It was a fresh approach to Woody's music which he originally recorded in the 1940's. The span of time in regards to the music we played was from 1939 with Woodchoppers Ball to 1949. We didn't do anything from the 50's. There were a few new things from the 60's but very few. Most of the stuff was very old like Good Earth, Apple Honey, and Caldonia. Good Earth was my favorite arrangement of all time. Snooky Young and I played that together one time and I asked him to let me know what he thought of this chart when we got through with it. He tapped me on the shoulder and said "that was the best arrangement I ever played Jake." I said same here! It's mostly ensemble playing. There are only a few bars of jazz in it. The last chorus is dynamite! Woody did it originally in 1944 with Dave Tough.

It was an easy band to play with Woody's band was. You really didn't have to fight anybody's time feel. The band played perfect time. I didn't have to fight to keep the tempo up, or play backbeats to keep this guy in time. Bill Chase would drill it into everyone's head "think time wise". Think time wise, get everything in place rhythmically, and everything else will fall into place. You can hear more clearly when everything is in time. You don't have to worry about the rhythm playing this and the band doing that. It makes everything wide open to blow over.

Some of the arrangements I had to read at first, some of the newer things. The older arrangements I knew as a kid. I used to practice to them. I learned them from the records and knew them long before I joined the band. Nat Pierce re-worked some of the older tunes to make them last longer than the original three minute version. One tune, I think it was Apple Honey; he reworked it and opened it up. That lasted 27 minutes and 47 seconds. That's a long time to play that fast. Sal Nistico must have played 90 choruses on it.

I think Thelonious Monk put it best when he said a drummer needs to swing as strong and as long as you can, even if it's only for four bars. When I'm playing time, I think about each beat I'm playing on the ride cymbal. I try to meld my ride cymbal sound with the sound of the acoustic bass. The whole idea of playing drums in a rhythm section and achieving a swing feel is to make that ride cymbal sound like it's playing the bass strings and the bass strings should sound like they're playing the ride cymbal. That's how close you got to get. The best examples to listen to for this conception are the old Miles Davis recordings with Percy Heath and Kenny Clarke. They sound like one guy. It sounds like each guy is playing the other guy's instrument. I phrase my cymbal beat in triplet form. When you get a little faster, it moves into more of a boogie woogie shuffle where the eighth notes are a little straighter. At an up-tempo like Caldonia, the eighth notes go almost completely straight. At that fast tempo, you need to accent beats one and three on the ride cymbal and it will come off sounding like 4/4 time. Shelly Manne was a master at that type of up tempo ride cymbal phrasing. The best I ever heard. You don't want to accent the two and the four on the ride cymbal at that speed. Besides, the hi-hat is already giving you that accent on the weak beats of each measure. Put some weight on beats one and three of your ride cymbal at those up tempos and your beat will come out as a nice and even solid 4 feeling.

The drummer in a big band lifts up the anchor and the horns should take care of themselves. The band should be swinging without the rhythm section. Benny Goodman would rehearse his band without the rhythm section, and especially without the drummer. He made the band swing by itself, and then when the rhythm came in and it wasn't swingin', he'd knew who to fire right away. That's why I love Gene Krupa so much. Gene would listen to the band and jump in right away and knew what to do.

Jake Hanna

Drummer	Artist	Title	Date	Label
Dee Barton	Stan Kenton	Adventures in Time	1962	Capitol
Louie Bellson	Louie Bellson	Skin Deep	1955	Norgran
	Various Artists	Hi-Fi Drums	1955	Capitol
	Louie Bellson	Concerto for Drums	1956	Norgran
	Louie Bellson	The Hawk Talks	1956	Norgran
	Louie Bellson	Swings Jules Styne	1960	Verve
	Ella Fitzgerald	Ella at Duke's Place	1965	Verve
	Louie Bellson	Their Time Was the Greatest	1995	Concord
Steve Bohannon	Don Ellis	Don Ellis at Monterey	1966	Blue Note
	Don Ellis	Live in 3 2/3/ 4 Time	1966	Pacific Jazz
	Don Ellis	Electric Bath	1967	Columbia
Jimmy Campbell	Stan Kenton	Standards in Silhouette	1959	Capitol
	Stan Kenton	Road Show Vol. 1	1959	Capitol
Frankie Capp	Bob Florence	Here and Now!	1965	Liberty
	Capp-Pierce	Juggernaut	1976	Concord
Sid Catlett	Louis Armstrong	Carnegie Hall Concert	1947	Ambassador
Nick Ceroli	Bob Florence	Live at Concerts By The Sea	1979	Trend
	Bob Florence	Westlake	1981	Discovery
	Bob Florence	Soaring	1982	Bosco
	Bob Florence	Magic Time	1983	Trend
Kenny Clarke	Clarke-Boland	Handle With Care	1963	Atlantic
	Clarke-Boland	Live at Ronnie Scott's	1969	MPS
Cozy Cole	Lionel Hampton	The Complete Lionel Hampton	1937-41	Bluebird
Irv Cottler	Various Artists	Hi-Fi Drums	1955	Capitol
	Frank Sinatra	Ring a Ding Ding	1960	Reprise
	Frank Sinatra	Strangers in the Night	1966	Reprise

Peter Erskine	Stan Kenton	Kenton Plays Chicago	1974	Creative World
	Stan Kenton	Fire, Fury, and Fun	1974	Creative World
	Maynard Ferguson	New Vintage	1977	CBS
	Jaco Pastorius	The Birthday Concert	1981	Warner Bros.
	Bob Mintzer	Camouflage	1986	dmp
	Bob Mintzer	Departure	1992	dmp
	Kenny Wheeler	Music for Large & Small Ensembles	1990	ECM
	Patrick Williams	Sinatraland	1997	Capitol
	Peter Erskine	Behind Closed Doors, Vol. 1 (w/the WDR Big Band)	1997	Fuzzy Music
	Joni Mitchell	Both Sides Now	2000	Reprise
	Wayne Bergeron	You Call This A Living?	2002	Wag Records
	Randy and Michael Brecker w/WDR Big Band	"Some Skunk Funk"	2006	Telarc
	Bob Florence Limited Edition	Eternal Licks and Grooves	2006	MAMA
Sonny Greer	Duke Ellington	Live in Fargo, North Dakota	1940	Jazz Classics
Jeff Hamilton	Woody Herman	Road Father	1978	Century
	Clayton-Hamilton	Groove Shop	1989	Capri
	Clayton- Hamilton	Heart and Soul	1991	Capri
	Clayton-Hamilton	Absolutely!	1995	Lake St
	Clayton-Hamilton	Explosive!	1999	Quest
	Clayton-Hamilton	Shout Me Out!	2000	Fable
Jake Hanna	Woody Herman	1963	1962	Philips
	Woody Herman	Encore 1963-Live At Basin Street, West Hollywood	1963	Philips
	Woody Herman	1964	1963	Philips
	Woody Herman	Live at Harrah's Club Lake Tahoe, Nevada	1964	Philips
	Woody Herman	40th Anniversary Carnegie Hall Concert	1976	RCA
Steve Houghton	Bob Florence	Funupsmanship (live)	1993	MAMA
	Bob Florence	With All the Bells and Whistles	1995	MAMA
Gus Johnson	Count Basie	Class of 54	1954	Blacklion
	Count Basie	Complete Original American RCA-Victor Recordings	2000	Definitive
Harold Jones	Count Basie	Basie Straight Ahead	1967	GRP
	Count Basie	Standing Ovation, Live at the Tropicana	1969	MCA

Jo Jones	Count Basie	Basie At Newport	1957	Verve
	Count Basie	Complete Original American Decca Recordings	2000	Definitive
	Count Basie	Complete Original American RCA-Victor Recordings	2000	Definitive
Philly Joe Jones	Philly Joe Jones	Drums Around the World	1959	Riverside
Rufus Jones	Maynard Ferguson	The New Sounds of Maynard Ferguson and his Orchestra	1964	Fresh Sounds
Gene Krupa	Benny Goodman	Roll 'Em, Volume 1	1937	Columbia
	Benny Goodman	At Carnegie Hall Complete	1938	Columbia
	Gene Krupa	Drummin' Man	1938-49	Columbia
	Gene Krupa	Drummer Man	1956	Verve
	Benny Goodman	Sing, Sing, Sing	1987	Bluebird
Gene Krupa and Buddy Rich	Jazz at the Philharmonic	The Original Drum Battle	1952	Verve
Don Lamond	Woody Herman	Blowin' Up a Storm	1945-47	Columbia
	Quincy Jones	Birth of A Band Vol. 1	1959	Mercury
	Don Lamond	Off Beat Percussion	1962	Command
	Woody Herman	40th Anniversary Carnegie Hall Concert	1976	RCA
Stan Levy	Stan Kenton	New Concepts of Artistry in Rhythm	1952	Capitol
	Stan Kenton	23 Degrees North 82 Degrees West	1952	Natasha
	Stan Kenton	Portraits on Standards	1953	Creative World
	Various Artists	Hi-Fi Drums	1955	Capitol
Mel Lewis	Stan Kenton	Kenton in Hi Fi	1956	Capitol
	Bill Holman	In a Jazz Orbit	1958	VSOP
	Terry Gibbs	Dream Band Vol. 1	1958	Contemporary
	Marty Paich	Moanin'	1959	Discovery
	Terry Gibbs	Dream Band Vol 2, Sundown Sessions	1959	Contemporary
	Terry Gibbs	Dream Band Vol. 3, Flying Home	1959	Contemporary
	Terry Gibbs	Dream Band Vol. 4, Main Stem	1961	Contemporary
	Terry Gibbs	Dream Band Vol. 5, The Big Cat	1961	Contemporary
	Thad Jones/ Mel Lewis	Presenting Thad Jones-Mel Lewis and the Jazz Orchestra	1966	Solid State
	Thad Jones/ Mel Lewis	Live at the Village Vanguard	1967	Solid State

	Thad Jones/ Mel Lewis	Monday Night!	1968	Solid State
	Thad Jones/ Mel Lewis	Central Park North	1969	Solid State
	Thad Jones/ Mel Lewis	Live In Munich	1976	A&M
	Mel Lewis	Soft Lights and Hot Music	1988	Music Masters
	Mel Lewis	The Definitive Thad Jones Vol. 1	1989	Music Masters
	Mel Lewis	The Definitive Thad Jones Vol. 2	1990	Music Masters
Shelly Manne	Stan Kenton	Live at Cornell University	1951	Jazz Unlimited
	Quincy Jones	Go West, Man	1957	Fresh Sound
	Shelly Manne	Manne, That's Gershwin	1965	Capitol
Jerry McKenzie	Stan Kenton	Kenton Tropicana	1959	Capitol
	Stan Kenton	Adventures In Blues	1960	Capitol
	Stan Kenton	Adventures In Jazz	1961	Capitol
Ray McKinley	Glenn Miller	Glenn Miller Army Air Force Band	1943/44	RCA
Butch Miles	Count Basie	On The Road	1979	Pablo
Joe Morello	Joe Morello	Joe Morello	1989	Bluebird
Sonny Payne	Count Basie	Atomic Basie	1959	Verve
	Sinatra-Basie	Sinatra-Basie	1962	Reprise
	Sinatra-Basie	It Might As Well Be Swing	1964	Reprise
	Sinatra-Basie	Live at the Sands	1966	Reprise
	Count Basie	Live at the Sands (Before Frank)	1966	Reprise
Charlie Persip	Bill Potts	The Jazz Soul of Porgy and Bess	1959	Capitol
Buddy Rich	Various Artists	Hi-Fi Drums	1955	Capitol
	Buddy Rich	This One's For Basie	1956	Verve
	Sammy Davis Jr	The Sounds of 66 (live)	1966	Reprise
	Buddy Rich	Live at the Chez	1966	Pacific Jazz
	Buddy Rich	The New One	1967	Pacific Jazz
	Buddy Rich	Big Swing Face	1967	Pacific Jazz
	Buddy Rich	Mercy, Mercy	1968	Pacific Jazz
	Buddy Rich	Keep the Customer Satisfied	1970	Pacific Jazz
	Buddy Rich	Rich In London	1971	RCA
	Buddy Rich	The Roar of 74	1974	Groove Merchant
	Buddy Rich	Plays and Plays and Plays	1977	RCA
	Buddy Rich	WHAM!	2000	M Live

John Riley	Bob Mintzer	Only in New York	1994	dmp
	Vanguard Jazz Orchestra	Likety Split	1997	New World
	Bob Mintzer	Latin From Manhattan	1998	dmp
Mickey Roker	Duke Pearson	Introducing Duke Pearson's Big Band	1967	Blue Note
	Duke Pearson	Now Hear This	1968	Blue Note
Ed Soph	Woody Herman	Brand New	1971	Fantasy
	Woody Herman	Giant Steps	1973	Fantasy
	Clark Terry	Big Bad Band, Live at Buddy's Place	1976	Vanguard
Jack Sperling	Les Brown	Concert at the Hollywood Palladium	1954	Coral
Alvin Stoller	Billy May	Sorta-May	1954	Capitol
	Various Artists	Hi-Fi Drums	1955	Capitol
	Frank Sinatra	Come Fly with Me	1957	Capitol
	Dennis Farnon	Dennis Farnon	1957	RCA
	Frank Sinatra	Sinatra's Swingin' Session	1960	Capitol
Grady Tate	Quincy Jones	Walking In Space	1969	A & M
Dave Tough	Artie Shaw	The Complete Artie Shaw Vol. 6	1942-45	Bluebird
	Woody Herman	The Old Gold Radio Shows	1944	Hindsight
	Woody Herman	Blowin' Up A Storm	1945-47	Columbia
John Von Ohlen	Stan Kenton	Live at Redlands University	1970	Creative World
	Stan Kenton	Stan Kenton Today	1972	Phase 4
Chick Webb	Chick Webb	Bronzeville Stomp	1937	Jazz Archives
	Chick Webb	Spinnin' the Webb	1994	MCA
Shadow Wilson	Count Basie	Live at the Royal Roost	1948	Arpeggio
Sam Woodyard	Duke Ellington	Live At Newport	1956	Columbia
	Duke Ellington	All Star Road Band Vol. 1	1957	Collectibles
	Duke Ellington	And His Mother Called Him Bill	1967	Bluebird
Ronnie Zito	Woody Herman	My Kind of Broadway	1965	Columbia
	Woody Herman	Woody's Winners	1965	Columbia
	Woody Herman	East And West	1967	Columbia

Drum Methods Discograhy

Hand Development Studies

Stick Control   George Lawrence Stone
Accents and Rebounds   George Lawrence Stone
Master Studies   Joe Morello
Roll Control   Andy White

Snare Drum Reading

Progressive Steps to Syncopation   Ted Reed
Podemski's Snare Drum Method   Benjamin Podemski
Modern Drum Studies   Simon Sternburg
Modern Reading Text in 4/4   Louie Bellson
The All American Drummer   Charley Wilcoxon
Modern Rudimental Swing Solos   Charley Wilcoxon
Portraits in Rhythm   Anthony Cirone

Drum Set Reading

Studio and Big Band Drumming   Steve Houghton
Drum Set Reading Anthology   Steve Houghton
The Big Band Drummer   Ron Spagnardi
It's Time for the Big Band Drummer   Mel Lewis and/Clem DeRosa
I've Got You Under My Skins   Irv Cottler
Contemporary Drummer + 1   Dave Weckl
Ultimate Play-Along for Drums   Dave Weckl
Their Time Was the Greatest   Louie Bellson

Coordination

Advanced Techniques
for the Modern Drummer   Jim Chapin
Drumset Essentials   Peter Erskine
Essential Techniques for Drum Set   Ed Soph
The New Breed   Gary Chester
Advanced Concepts   Kim Plainfield
Future Sounds   David Garibaldi
The Drummers Complete Vocabulary   John Ramsey

Style

Essential Styles Vols. 1 and 2	Steve Houghton
The Art of Bop Drumming	John Riley
Beyond Bop	John Riley
The Drum Perspective	Peter Erskine
New Orleans Jazz and	
Second Line Drumming	Herlin Riley/and Johnny Vidacovich
Afro-Cuban Rhythms for Drum Set	Frank Malabe/Bob Weiner
Brazilian Rhythms for Drum Set	Duduka Da Fonseca/Bob Weiner
Funkifying the Clave	Airto Moreira/and Dan Thress
Conversations in Clave	Horacio El Negro Hernandez

Photography Credit

Louie Bellson	(page 179)
Charles Braun	(page 217)
Carmen G. Campagnoli	(page 205)
Leonard Cuddy	(pages 96, 199, 220, 234)
Danny Gottlieb	(page 223)
Stanley Kay	(pages 220, 237)
Jim Lackey	(page 231)
Kenny Rittenhouse	(page 57)
Zildjian	(pages 140, 174, 200, 204, 209, 213, 221, 240)

Steve Fidyk

Jazz drummer, author, and educator Steve Fidyk has toured and recorded with Maureen McGovern, New York Voices, Cathy Fink and Marcy Marxer, The Capitol Bones, The Taylor/Fidyk Big Band, an ensemble he co-leads with Stan Kenton arranger Mark Taylor, and is currently the drummer with the Army Blues Jazz Ensemble from Washington D.C.

As a leader, Fidyk's discography includes: *Big Kids* (U.S. Roots), *A Perfect Match* (Write Groove), and *Live at Blues Alley* (OA2) and can be heard on over 50 recordings as a contributing artist.

As an educator, Fidyk has authored the following Mel Bay books: *The Drum Set SMART Book, Inside the Big Band Drum Chart, Jazz Drum Set Independence 3/4, 4/4, and 5/4 Time Signatures,* and an instructional DVD entitled *Set Up and Play*! For information on these methods, please visit **www.melbay.com.**

He has also recorded over 75 jazz play-along volumes for the Hal Leonard Corporation and contributed drum transcriptions to Drum Standards and Peter Erskine's The Drum Perspective.

Fidyk has served on the faculty at Wilkes University, St. Mary's College of Maryland, George Mason University and The University of Maryland and is presently a member of the jazz faculty at Temple University in Philadelphia, Pennsylvania. He holds a Masters Degree in Jazz Studies from the University of Maryland and Bachelors in Music Education from Wilkes University.

Steve Fidyk endorses Ludwig Drums, Zildjian Cymbals, Vater Drumsticks, Remo Drumheads, DW Pedals, and Latin Percussion products.

For more information, please visit **www.stevefidyk.com**